José Luis Morales • Laura Miller • Tessa Lochowski
Series advisor: David Nunan

Pearson Education Limited
Edinburgh Gate
Harlow
Essex CM20 2JE
England
and Associated Companies throughout the world.

Poptropica English

Based on the work of Tessa Lochowski

Phonics syllabus and activities by Rachel Wilson

Editorial and project management by hyphen

First published 2015
Seventeenth impression 2024

ISBN: 978-1-292-11244-2

Set in Fiendstar 17/21pt

Printed in Slovakia by Neografia

Illustrators: Adam Clay, Leo Cultura, Joelle Dreidemy (Bright Agency), Tom Heard (Bright Agency), Andrew Hennessey, Marek Jagucki, Sue King, Stephanine Lau, Daniel Limon (Beehive Illustration), Katie McDee, Bill Mcguire (Shannon Associates), Baz Rowell (Beehive Illustration), Jackie Stafford, Olimpia Wong, Teddy Wong and Yam Wai Lun

Contents

1 Look and write the alphabet.

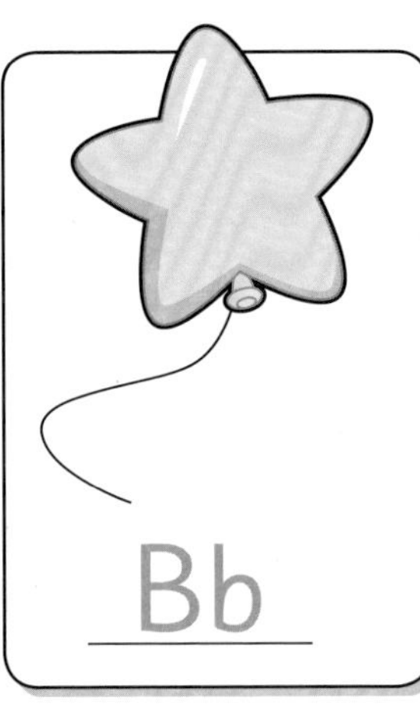

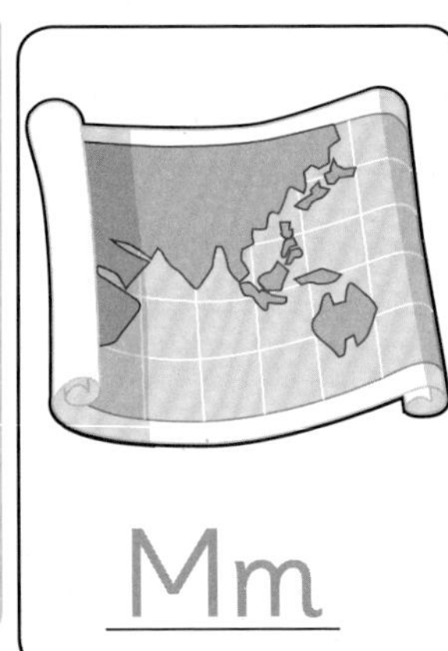

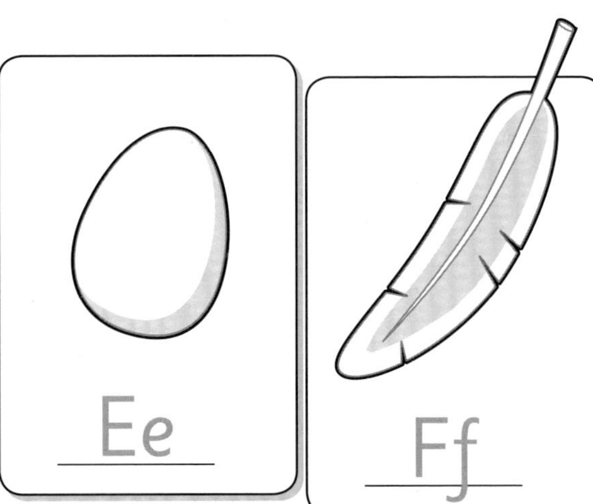

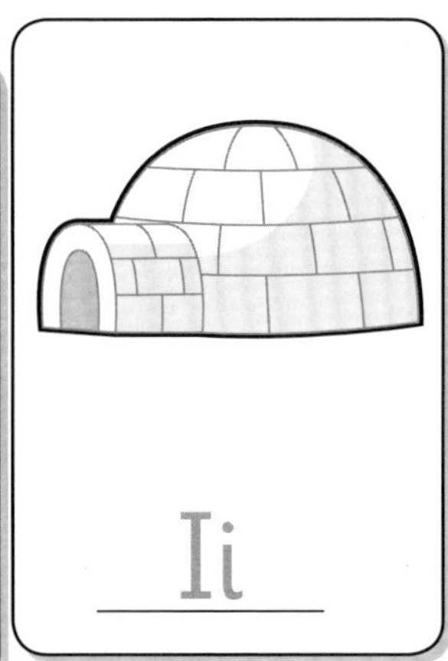

02 **Sing.** (See Student Book page 7.)

1 Match and write.

Beth Cody Waldo Harry

2 Write. Then color.

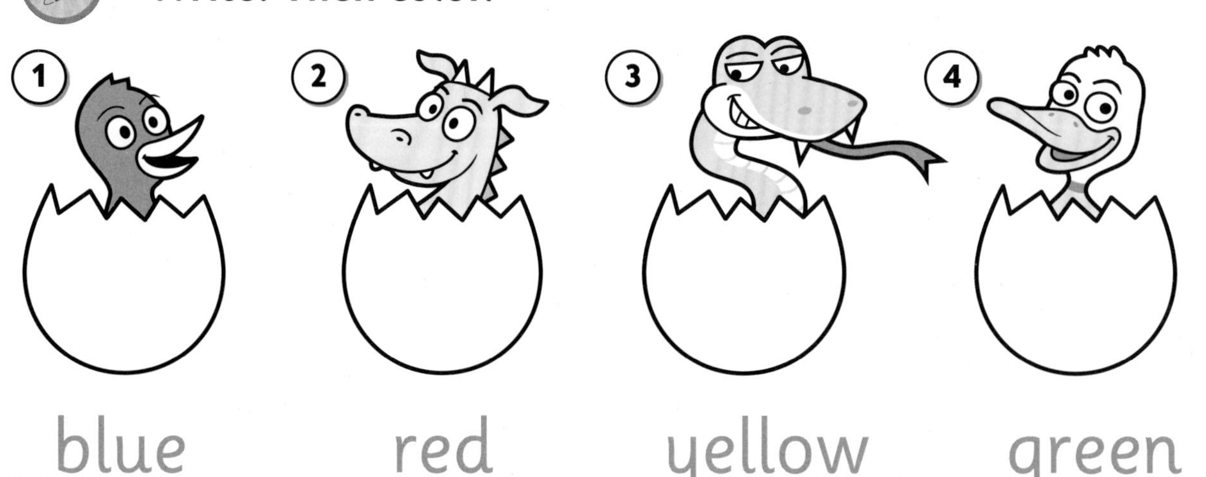

blue red yellow green

3 Draw and color.

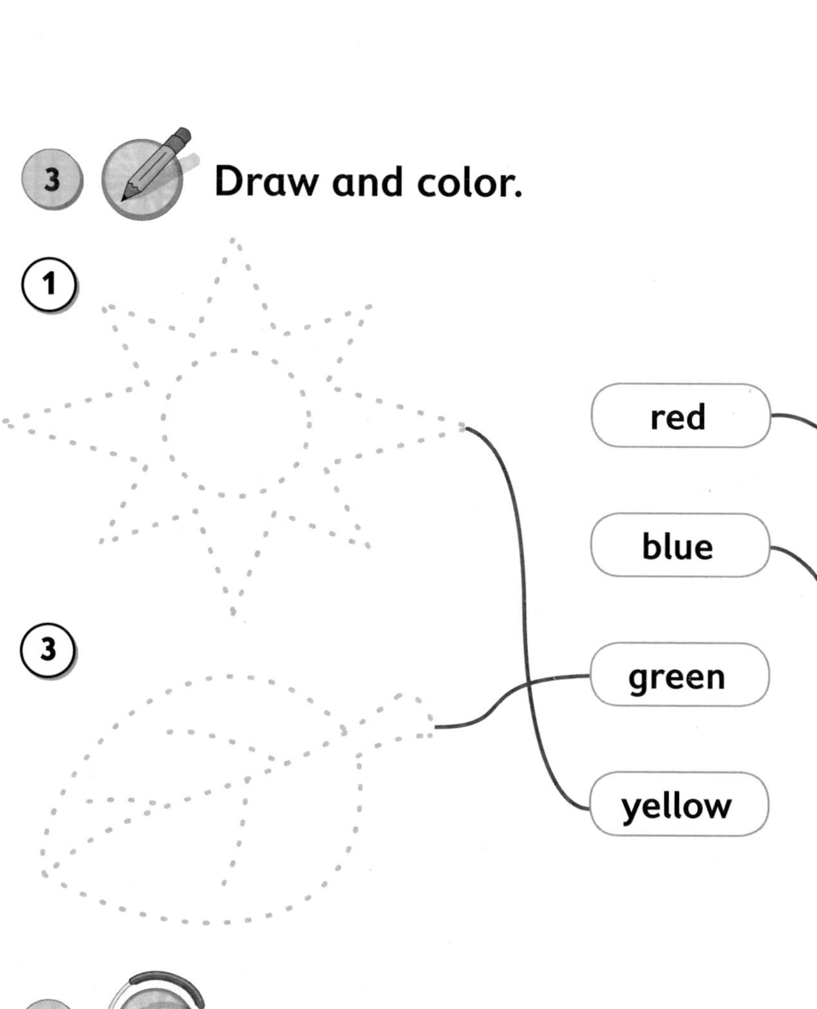

4 Listen and check (✓). Then color.

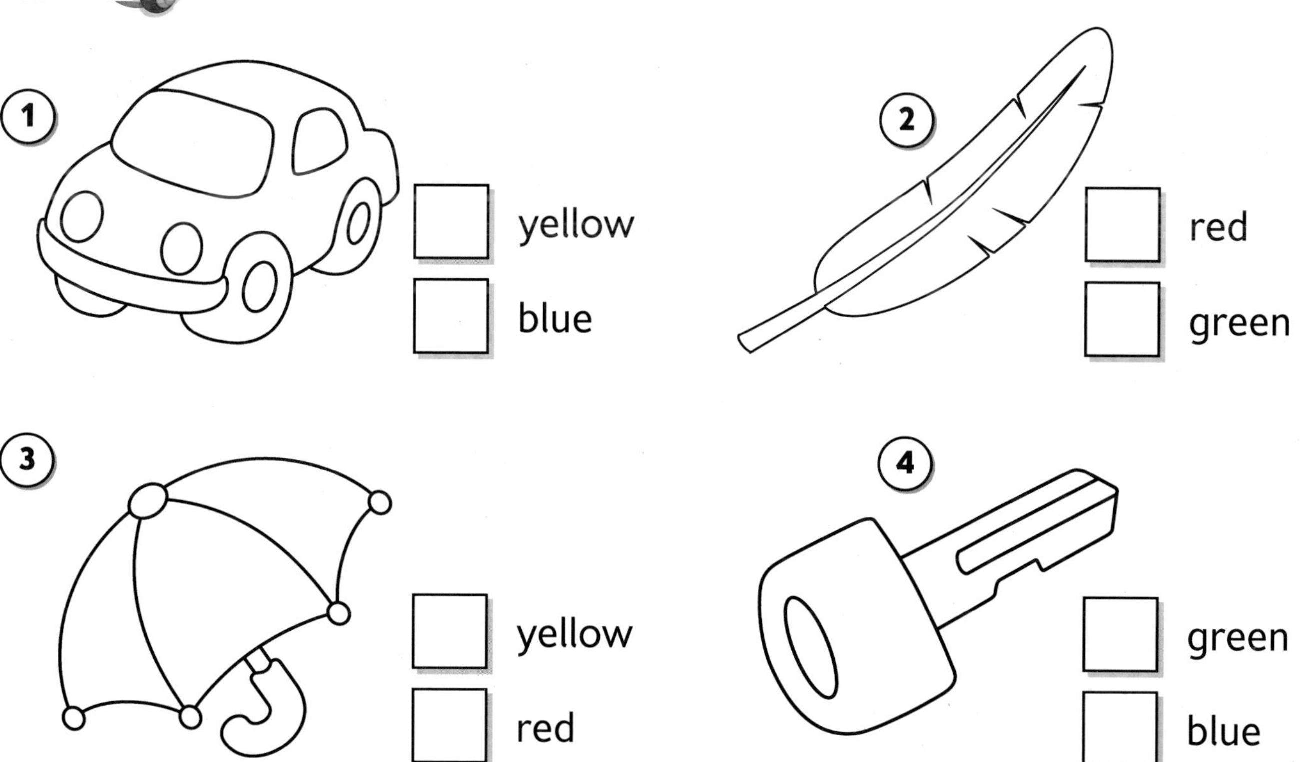

5 Write. Then count and match.

0 → ___ → ___ → 3 → ___ → 5

6 Write. Then count and match.

6 → ___ → 8 → ___ → 10

Lesson 3 05 **Chant.** (See Student Book page 10.)

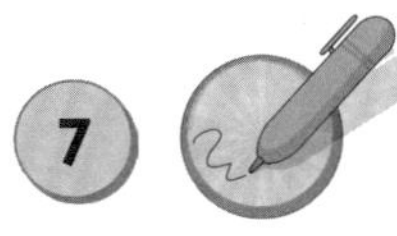

7 Look and match.

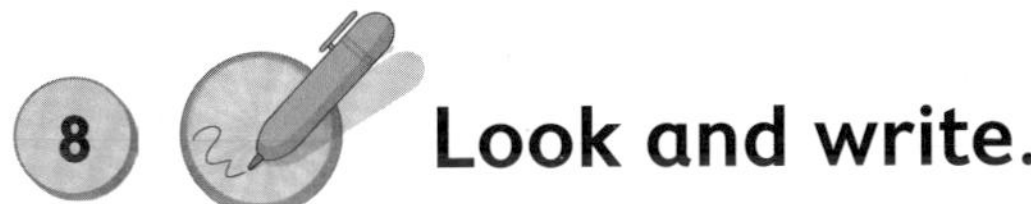

8 Look and write.

Are you ready for Unit 1?

1 My birthday

1 Write and color.

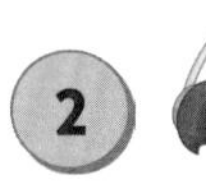  Listen and number.

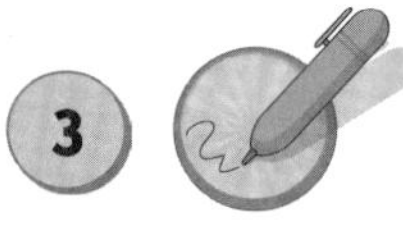 Look and write.

1 I'm two.

2 I'm four.

3 I'm ten.

4 I'm seven.

4 Write and match.

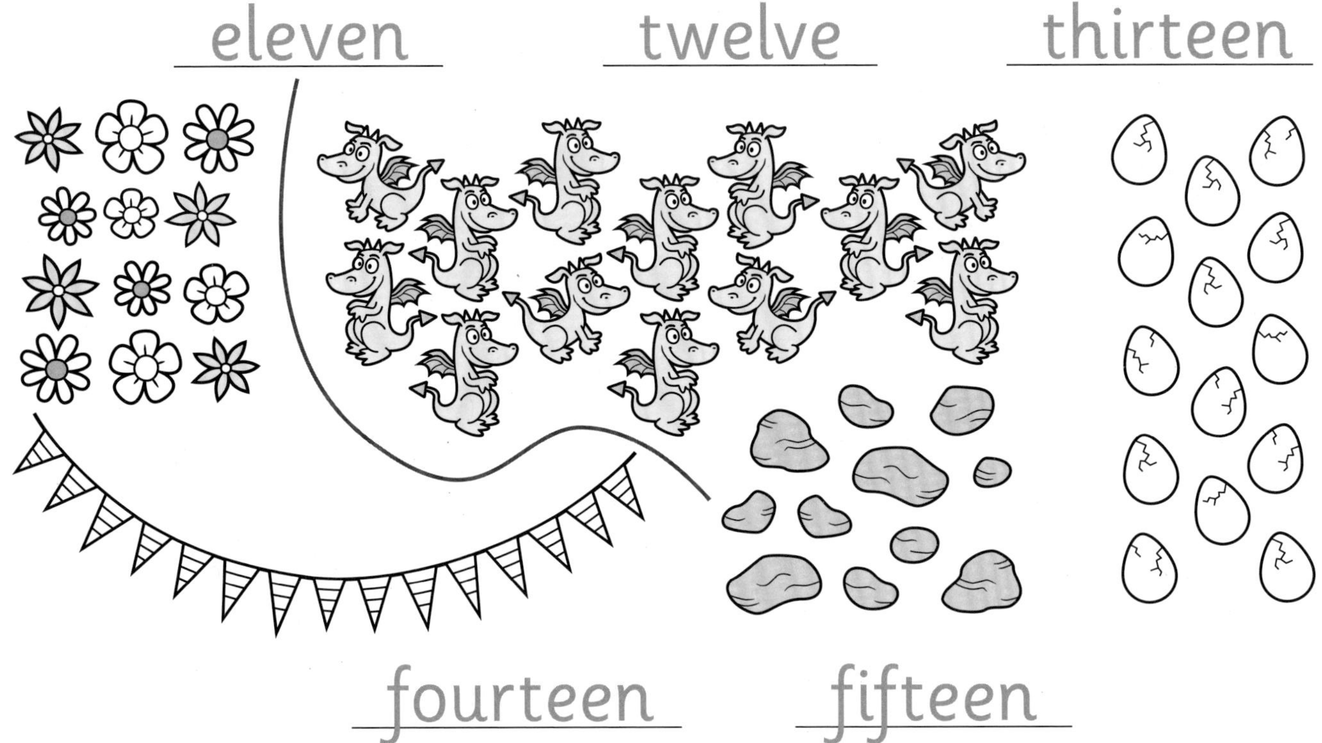

5 Circle. Then listen and number.

 Sing. (See Student Book page 14.)

 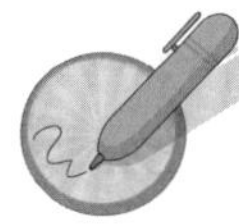

Read and write. Then color.

1

What color is it?

It's orange.

2

What color is it?

It's purple.

3

Is it brown?

Yes, it is.

4

Is it red?

No, it isn't. It's pink.

7 Listen and color.

1

2

3

4

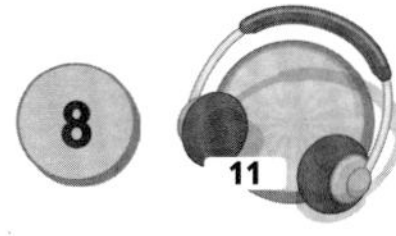
8 Listen and circle. Then color.

1

a 

b 

2

a 

b 

3

a 

b 

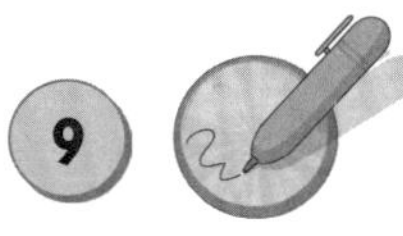
9 Count and write.

a 

b 

c 

d 

VALUES

It's good to share.

  **Look, share, and draw.**

 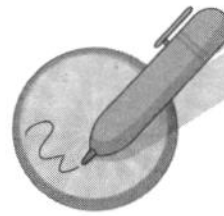 **Draw and write.**

I share with my ____________________.

12 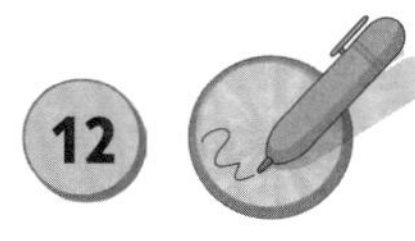 **Match. Then write.**

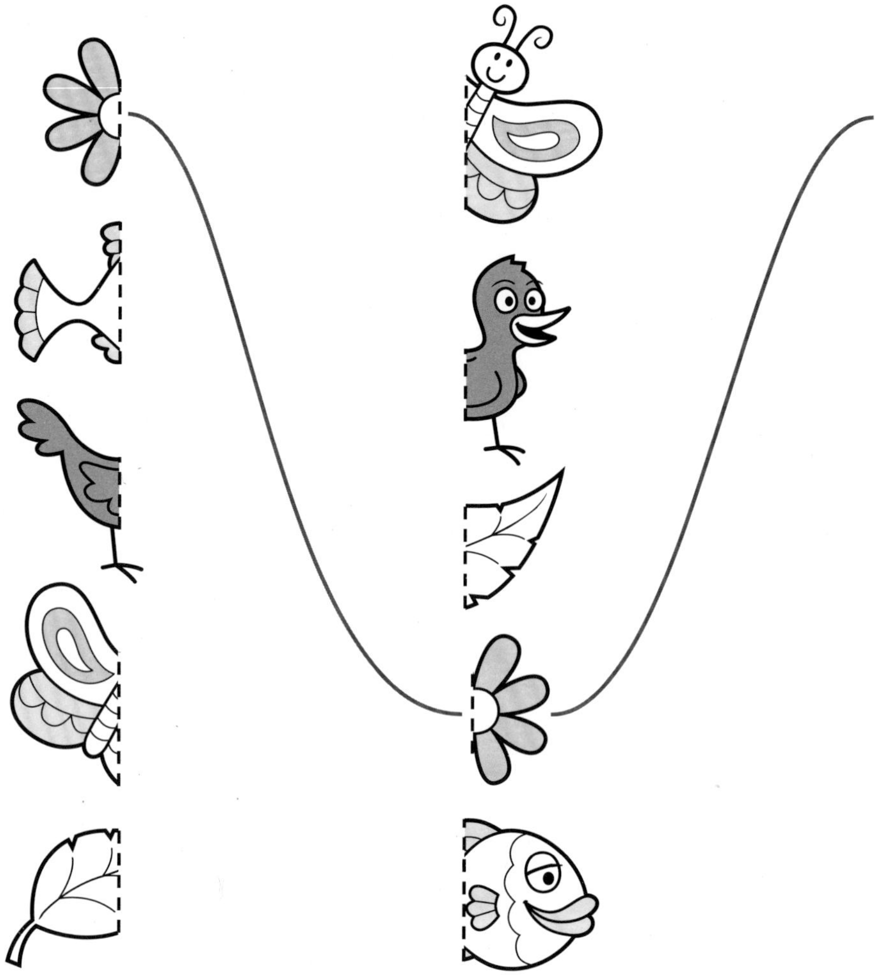

1 flower

2 butterfly

3 leaf

4 fish

5 bird

13  **Color. Then circle.**

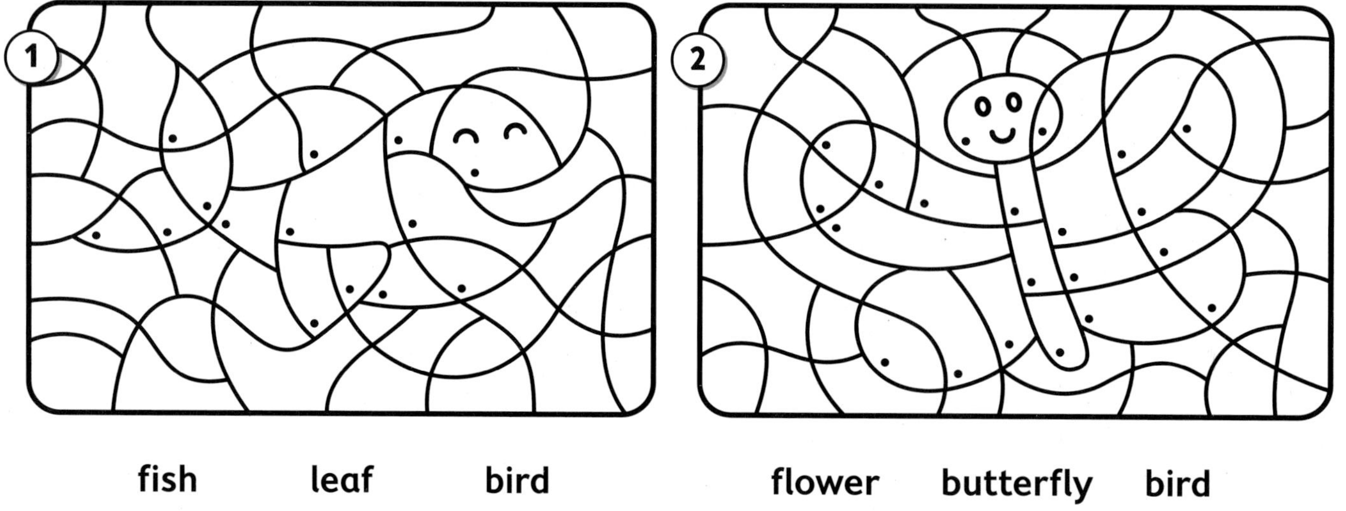

1 fish leaf bird

2 flower butterfly bird

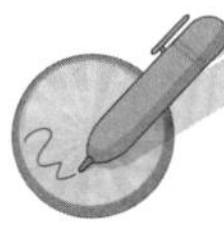

Read the words. Circle the pictures.

PHONICS
a p s t

pat tap

15 Listen to the sounds and circle the letters.

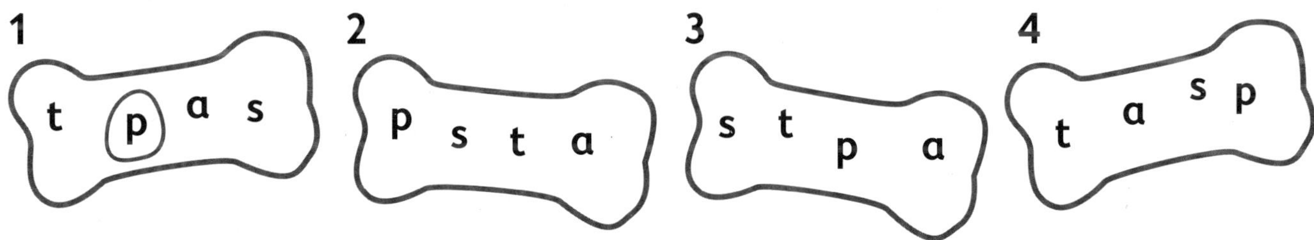

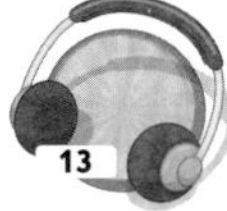

16 Listen and write the letters.

1 t 2 ____ 3 ____ 4 ____

17 Listen and write the words.

1 s a t 2 __ a p 3 __ __ t 4 __ a t

  **Color. Then say.**

A butterfly! It's pink.

1	black
2	brown
3	blue
4	purple
5	pink
6	orange
7	green

 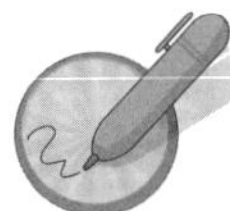 **Look and circle.**

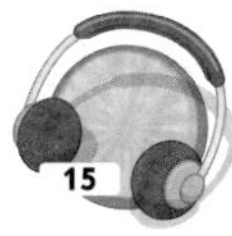

20 Listen and circle.

1

2

3

4

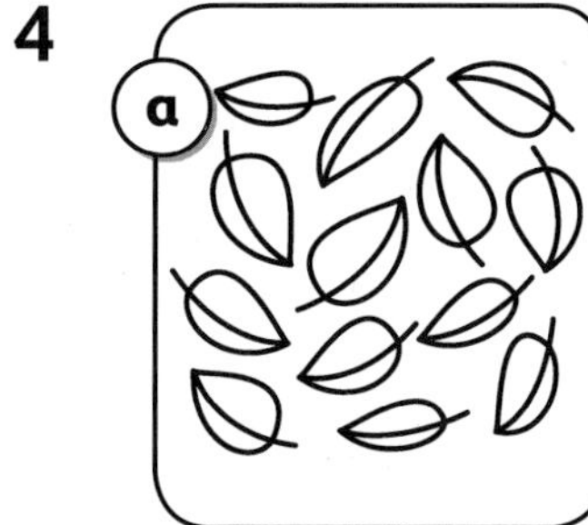

21 Draw.

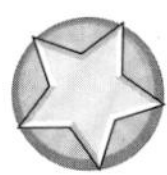

Are you ready for Unit 2?

2 At school

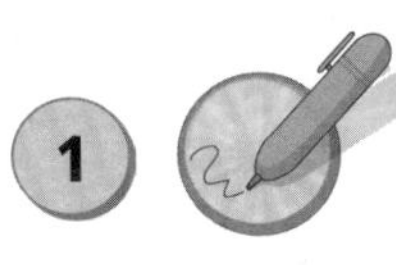

1 Draw. Then write.

1

eraser

2

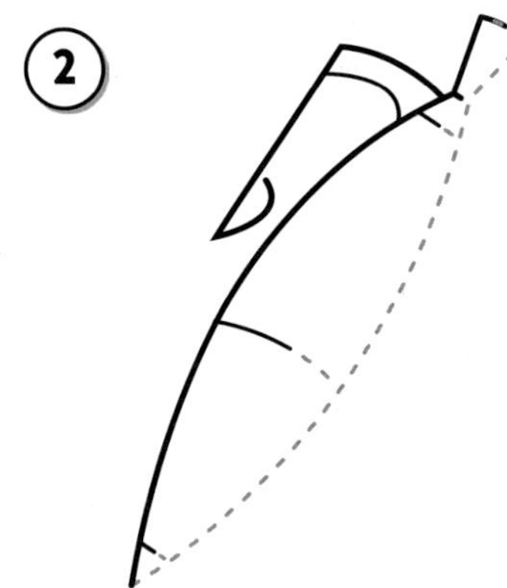

pen

3

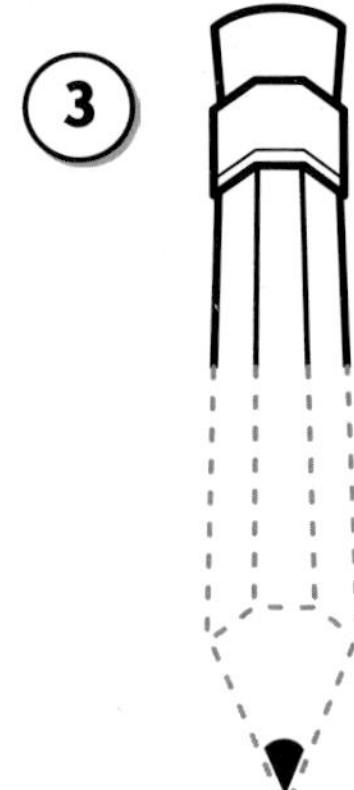

pencil

4

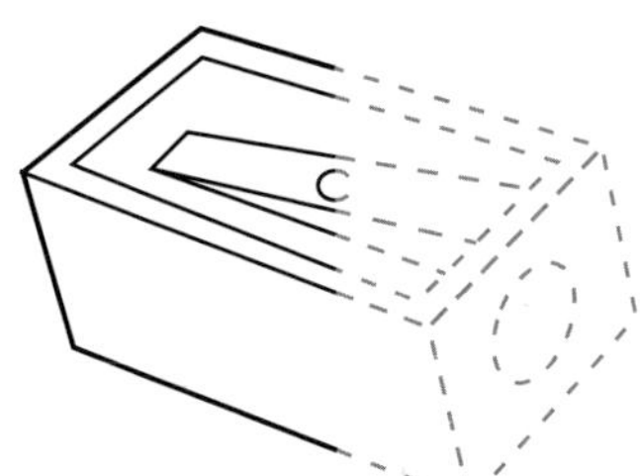

pencil sharpener

5

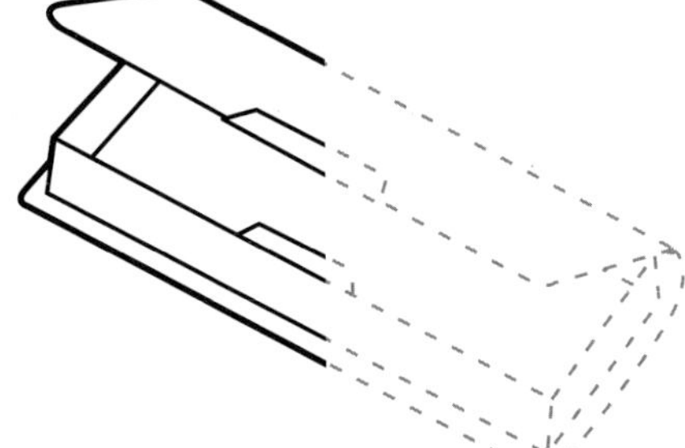

pencil case

6

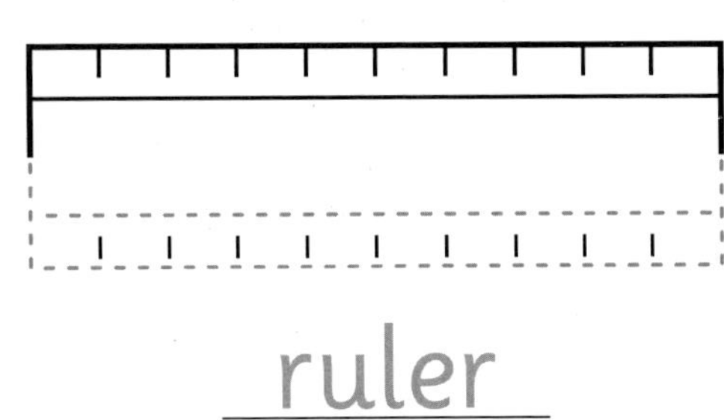

ruler

7

book

2 Listen, circle and color.

1

2

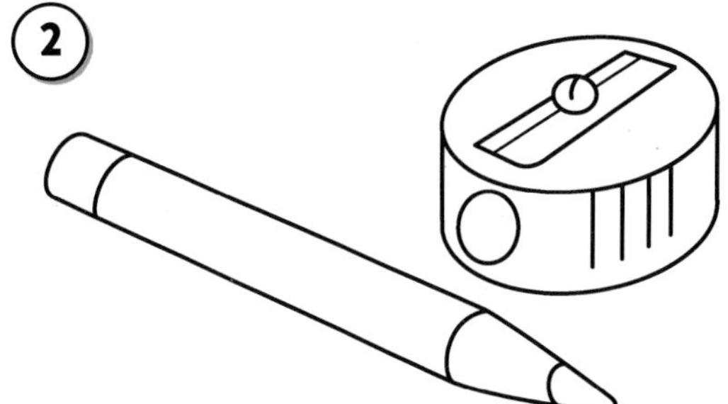

3

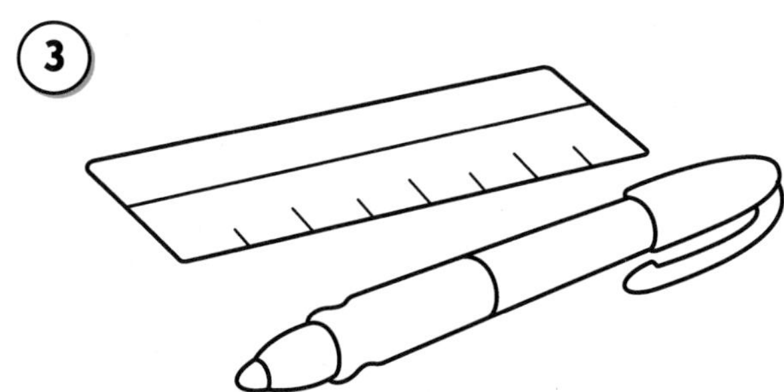

4

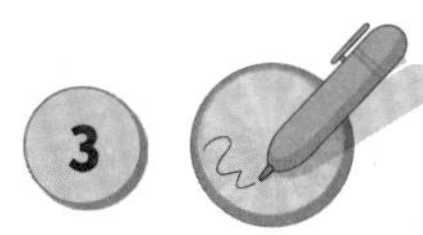

3 Write. Then read and check (✓).

1 It's a pencil sharpener.

2  It's a book.

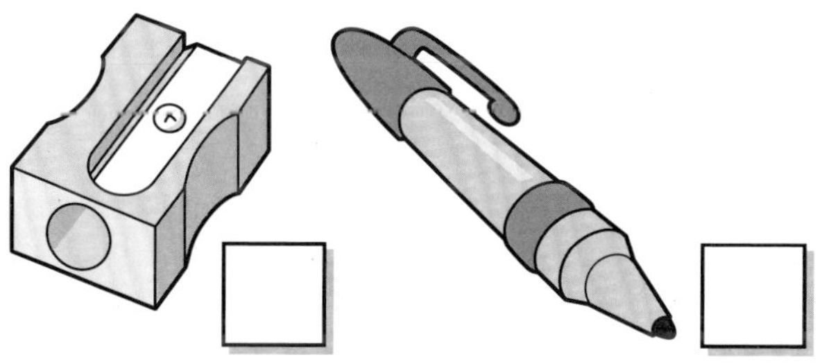

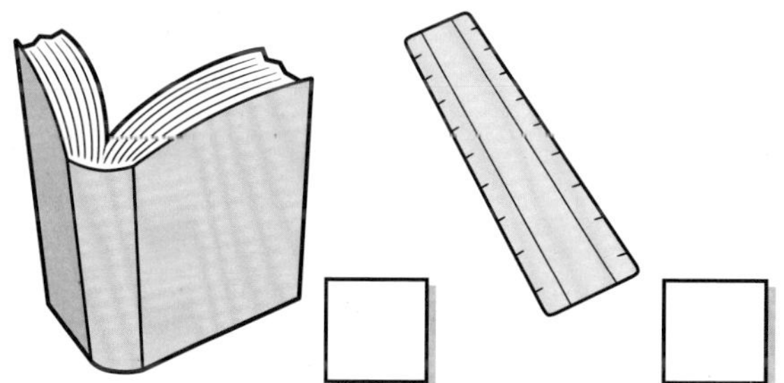

3 It's an eraser.

4  It's a pen.

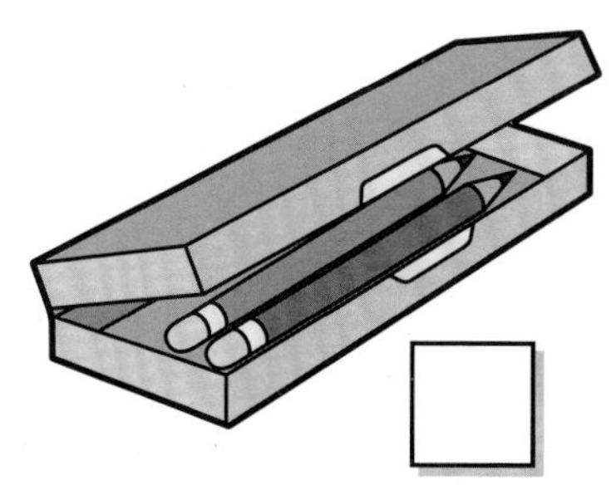

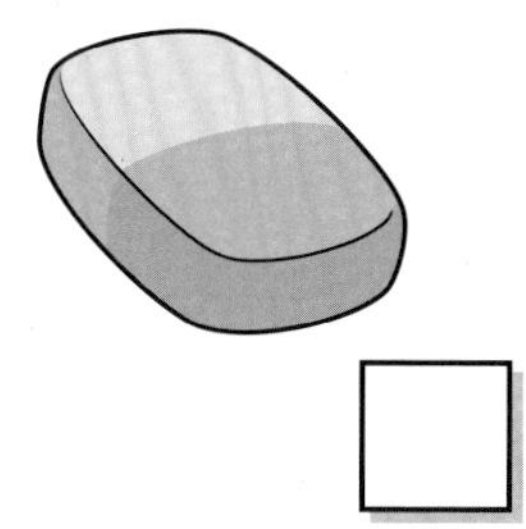

4 Match.

1 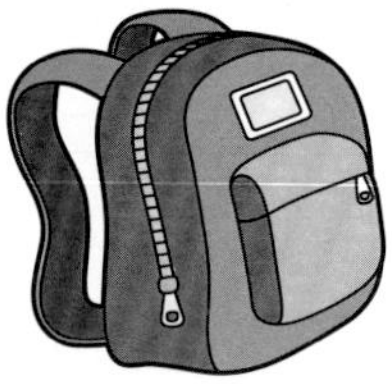

2 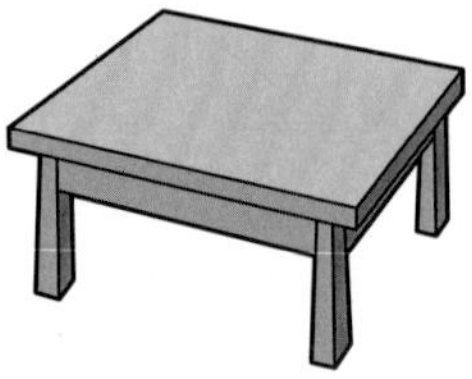

3 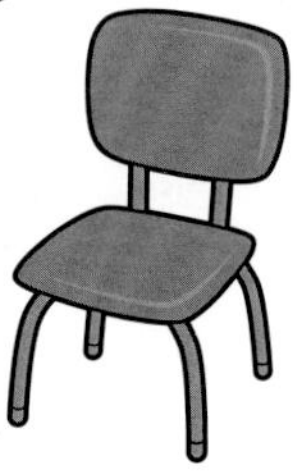

4

5 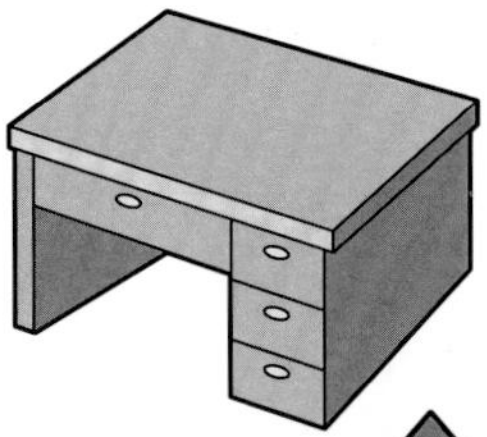

6 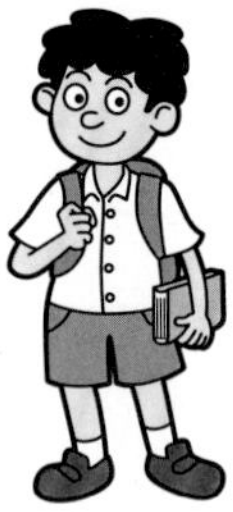

7 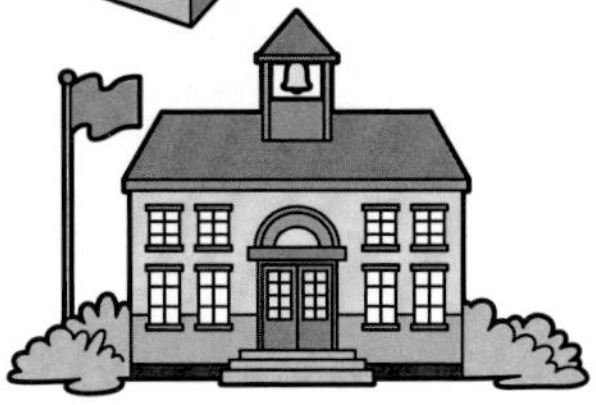

8 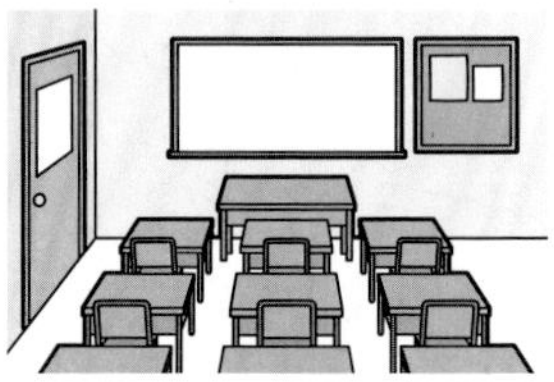

a chair

b desk

c board

d backpack

e school

f table

g classroom

h student

5 Count. Then write and circle.

1 **5** desk / (desks)

2 ☐ table / tables

3 ☐ backpack / backpacks

4 ☐ board / boards

5 ☐ chair / chairs

6 ☐ student / students

 18 **Sing.** (See Student Book page 24.)

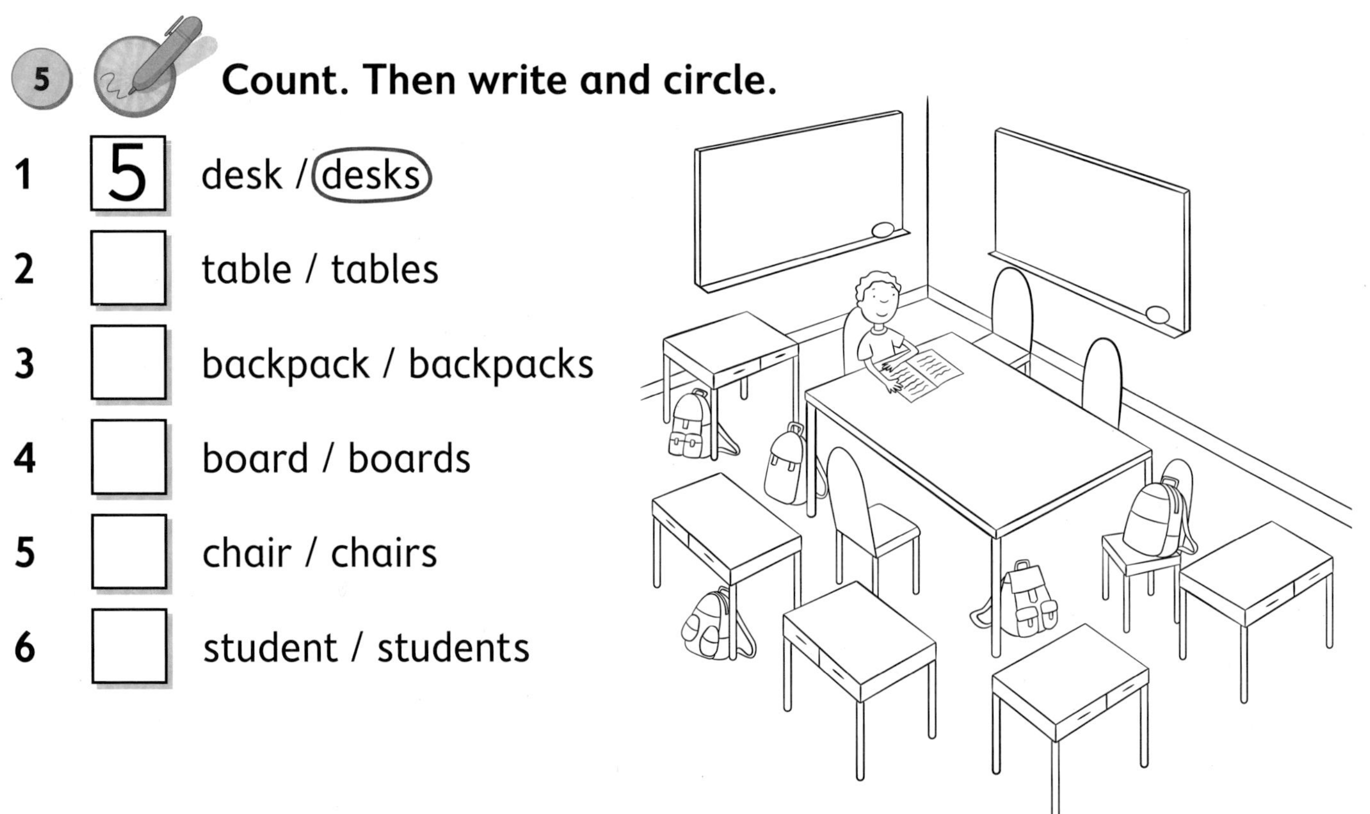

6 19 **Listen and match. Then color.**

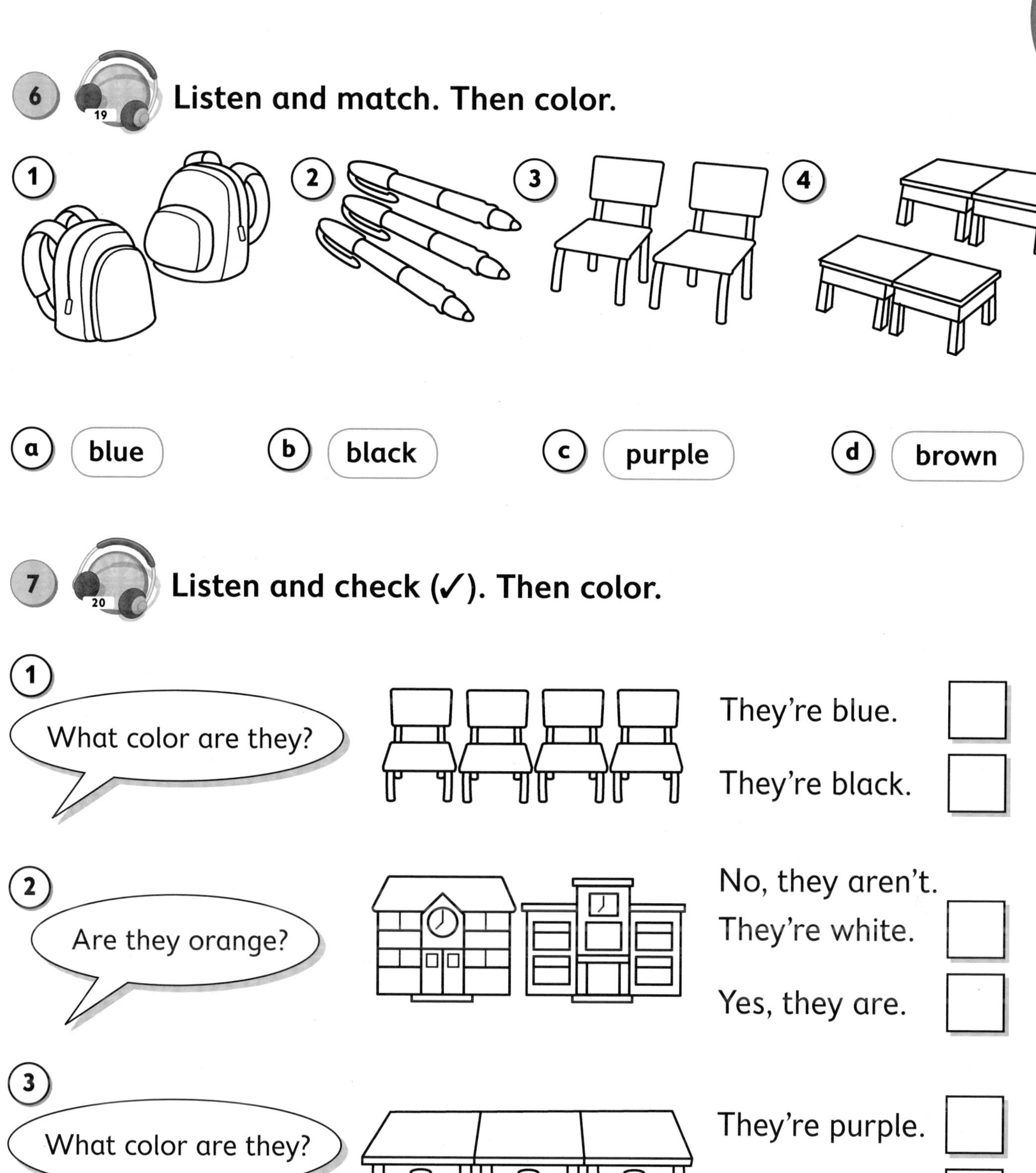

7 20 **Listen and check (✓). Then color.**

1 What color are they?
They're blue. ☐
They're black. ☐

2 Are they orange?
No, they aren't. They're white. ☐
Yes, they are. ☐

3 What color are they?
They're purple. ☐
They're pink. ☐

4 Are they gray?
Yes, they are. ☐
No, they aren't. ☐

Listen and number. Then color.

Draw. Then circle and color.

What's this?

It's a green (backpack / dragon).

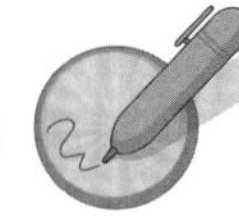

Look. Then ✓ or ✗.

BECKY

TOM

Becky tries hard at school. ☐

Tom tries hard at school. ☐

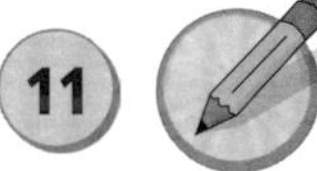

Draw.

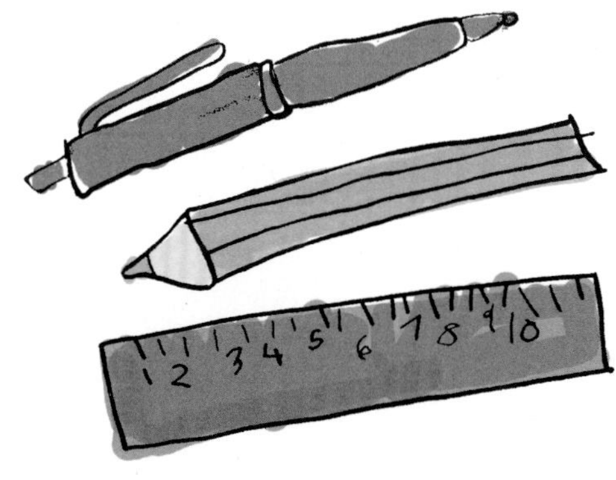

 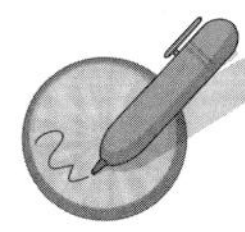 **Match and write.**

1 

2 

3 

4 

a 

b 

c 

d 

piano guitar drum violin

 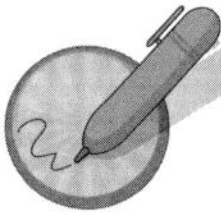 **Read and circle.**

1 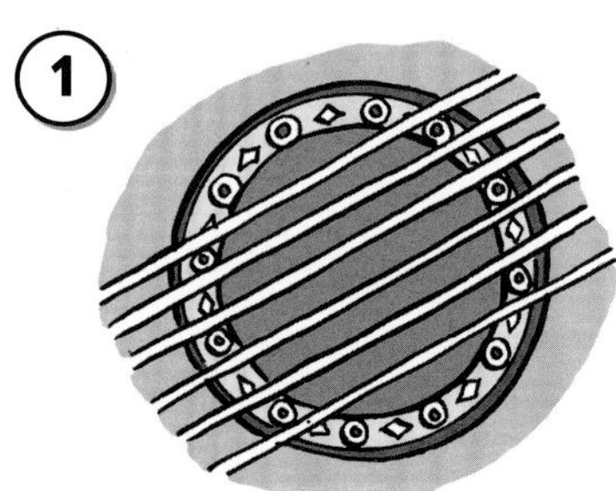

It's a (guitar / drum).

2 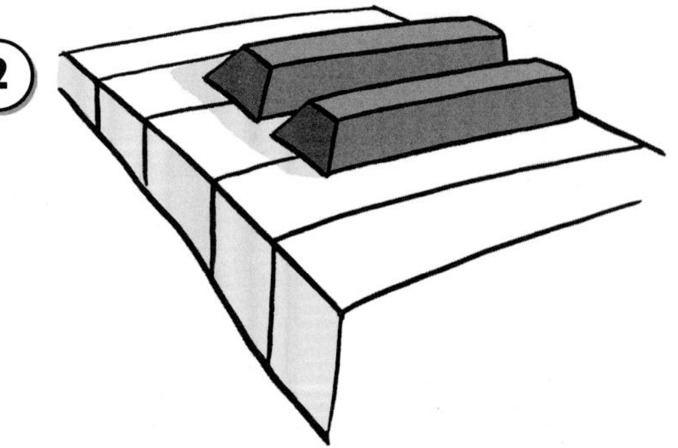

It's a (piano / violin).

3 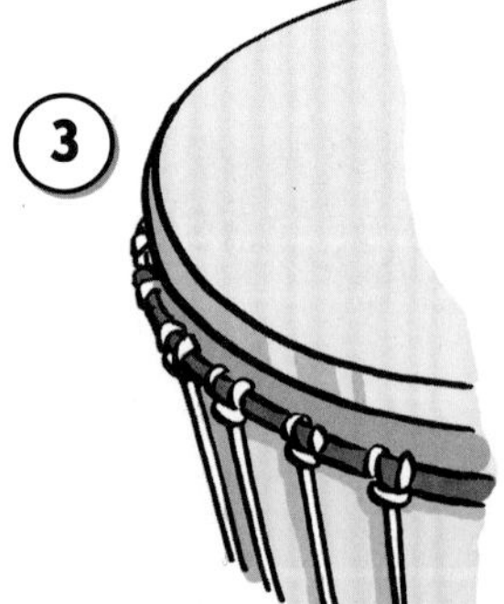

It's a (piano / drum).

PHONICS

d i m n

 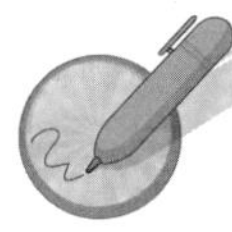 Read the words. Circle the pictures.

dip man nap pan

  Listen to the sounds and circle the letters.

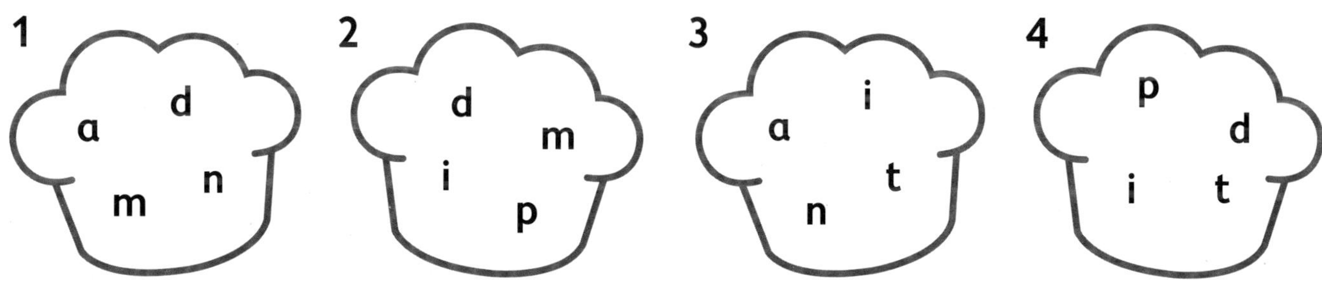

 Listen and write the letters.

1 ______ 2 ______ 3 ______ 4 ______

17 Listen and write the words.

1 s _ t 2 a _ 3 _ a n 4 _ t

Listen and circle.

1 

2 

3 

4 

19 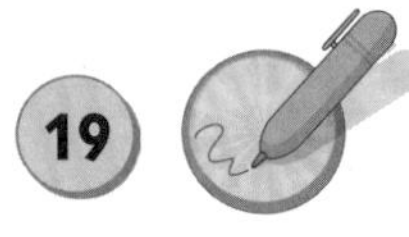

Read and match. Then color.

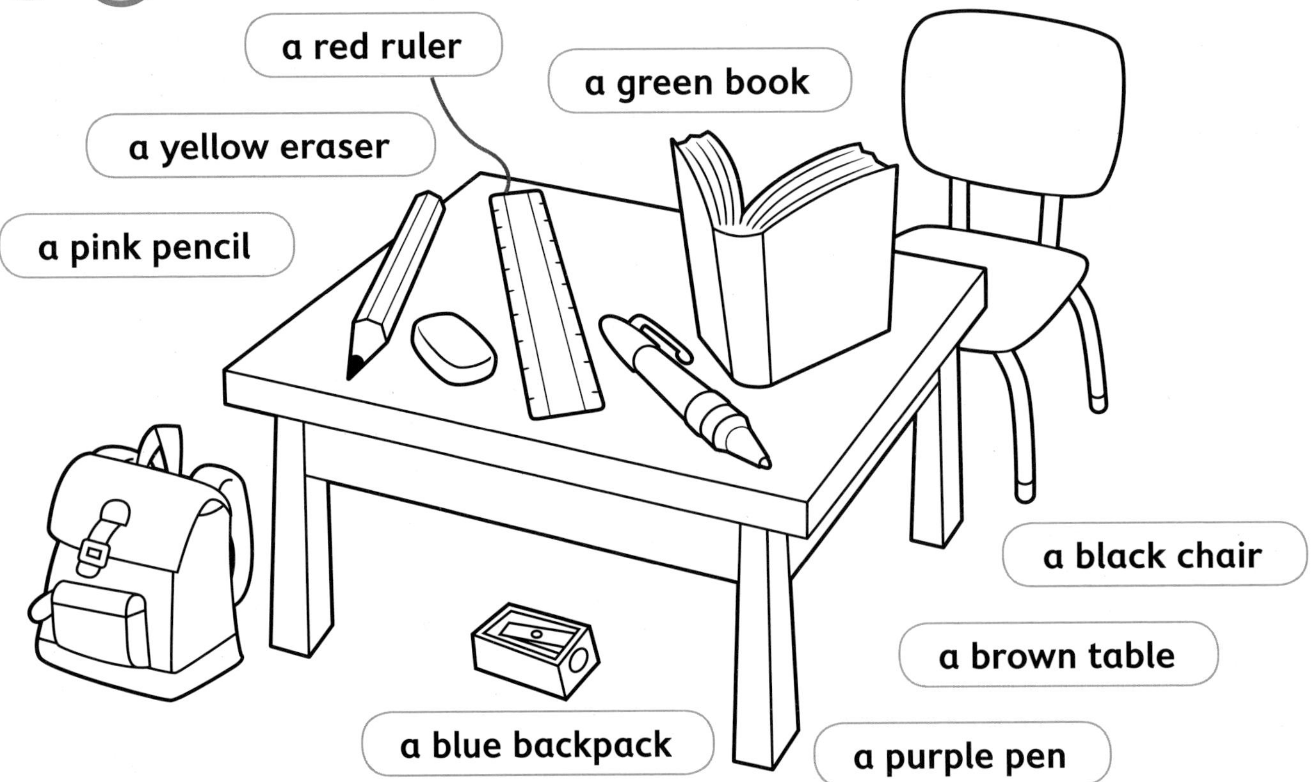

20 Listen and draw. Then listen again and color.

1 

2 

3 

4 

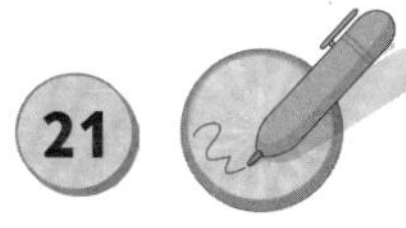

21 Find and count. Then write.

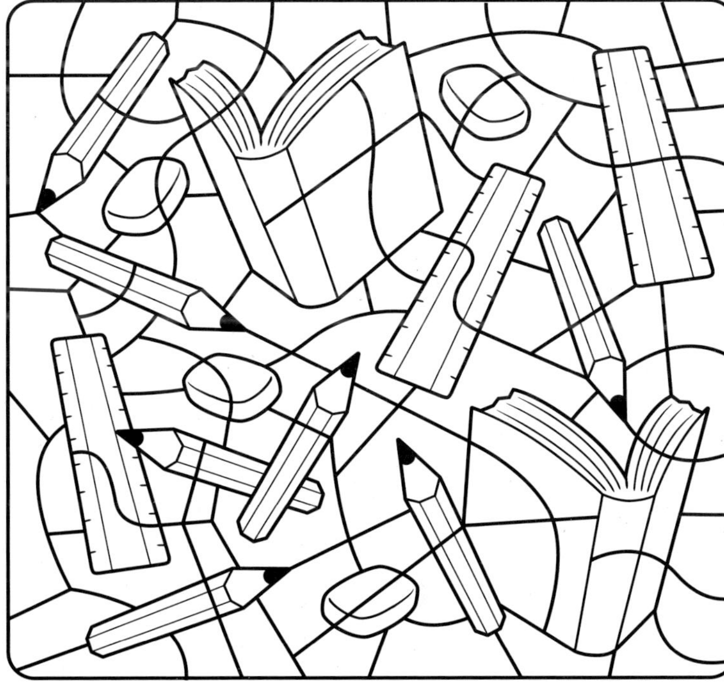

a [4] erasers

b [ ] pencils

c [ ] rulers

d [ ] books

Are you ready for Unit 3?

3 My family

1 Write and number.

1 mom
2 dad
3 grandfather

1

This is my family.

4 grandmother
5 sister
6 brother

 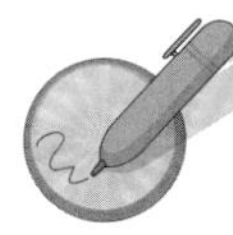 **Find and color. Then circle.**

This is my (mom / friend).
He's (nine / ten).

This is my (grandmother / sister).
She's (seven / eight).

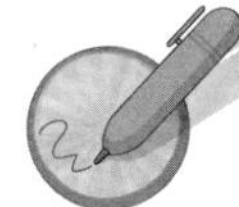 **Write and match.**

1 He's eight.

2 She's seven.

3 She's five.

4 He's ten.

 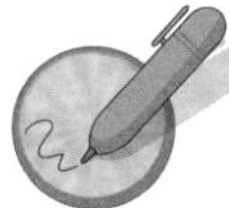

Look and number.

1	a vet	2	a pilot	3	a doctor	4	a teacher
5	a cook	6	an artist	7	a farmer	8	a dentist

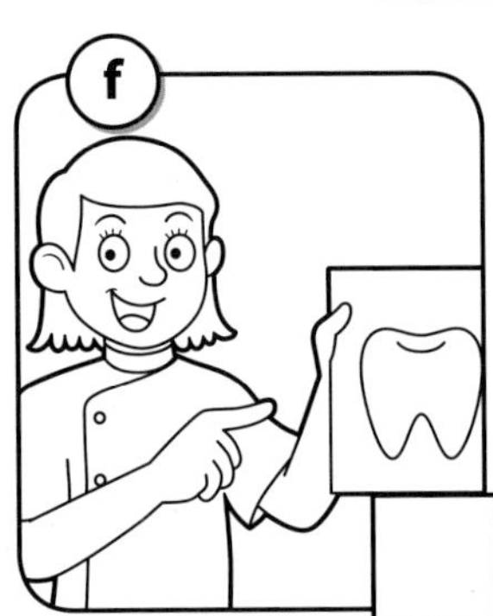

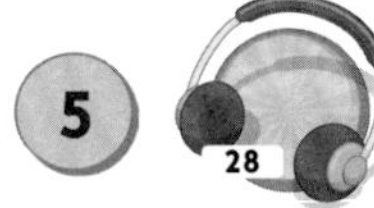

Listen and ✓ or ✗.

 29 **Sing.** (See Student Book page 36.)

6 Listen and circle.

1 a  b 

2 a  b 

3 a b 

4 a  b 

7 Write. Then check (✓).

1

Is he a cook?

a Yes, he is. ☐

b No, he isn't. ☐

2

Is she a doctor?

a Yes, she is. ☐

b No, she isn't. ☐

3

Is he an artist?

a Yes, he is. ☐

b No, he isn't. ☐

4

Is she a vet?

a Yes, she is. ☐

b No, she isn't. ☐

8
Find and circle.
STORY
1
This is my mom.
She's a dancer.
a
b
2
This is my dad.
He's a sailor.
a
b
3
This is my aunt.
She's a cook.
a
b
9
Write and match.
This is my sister.
She's six.
3
6
8

Love your family.

10 **Write and match.**

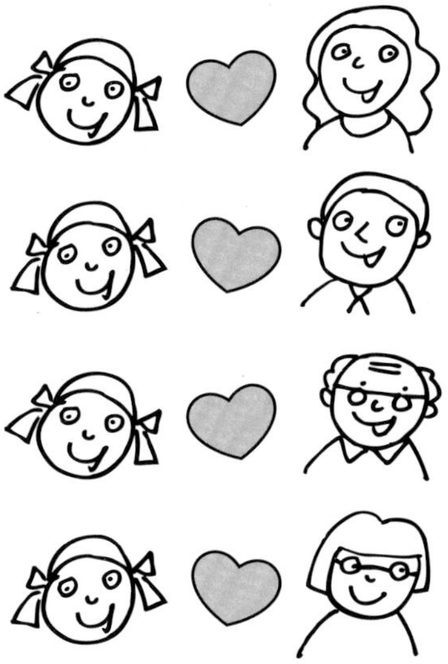

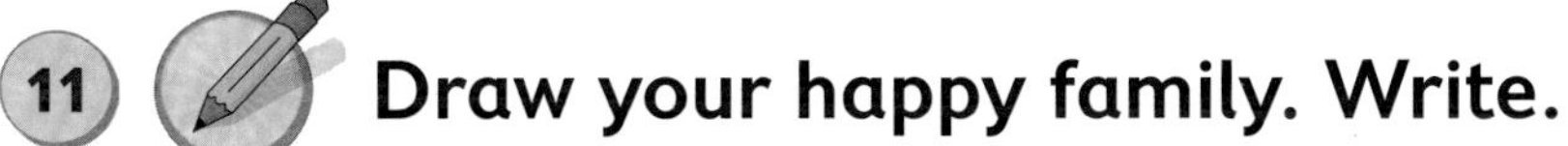

I love my mom.

I love my dad.

I love my grandmother.

I love my grandfather.

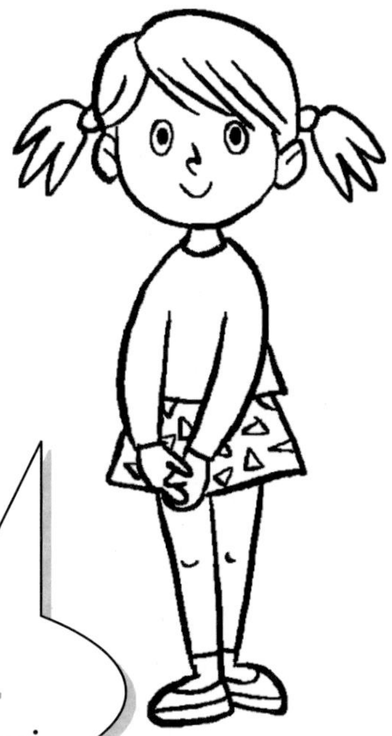

11 **Draw your happy family. Write.**

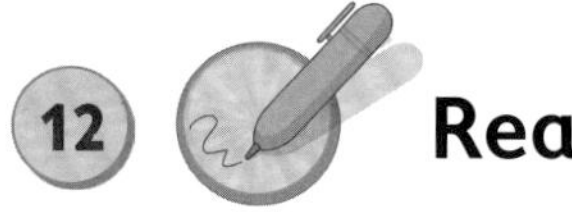

12 Read and match.

1 It's a collage.

2 It's a sculpture.

3 It's a painting.

4 It's a drawing.

a
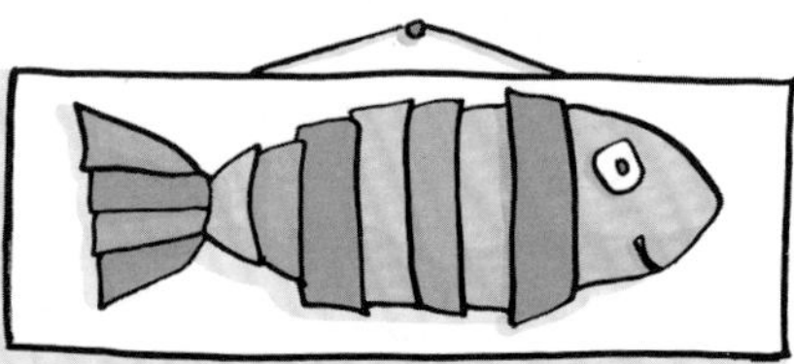

b

c

d

13 Color and circle.

1 = red 2 = yellow 3 = orange 4 = green 5 = brown

It's a (painting / collage). It's a (bird / butterfly).

PHONICS

c g o

 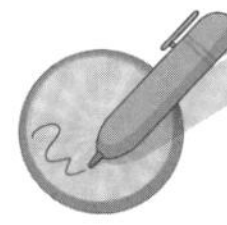 Read the words. Circle the pictures.

can cap dig dog

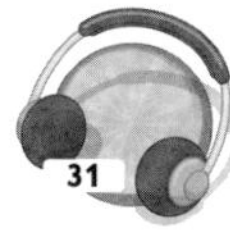 15 Listen to the sounds and circle the letters.

1 g c o t

2 c o g a

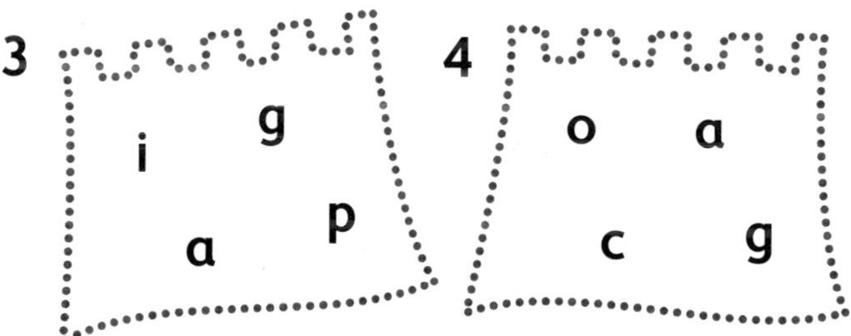

 16 Listen and write the letters.

1 ________ 2 ________ 3 ________

 17 Listen and write the words.

1 __ a s 2 __ a t 3 __ __ n 4 t __ p

 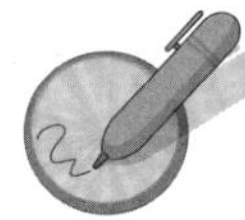

18 Read and match. Then write.

1 dad

2 mom

3 grandmother

4 grandfather

5 sister

6 brother

19 Listen and check (✓).

1

a 

b 

2

a 

b 

3

a 

b 

4

a 

b 

 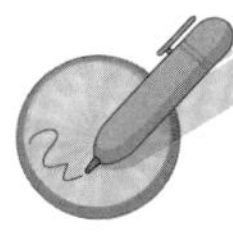 Match. Then write.

1  2  3  4

a She's a vet.

b He's a pilot.

c He's a teacher.

d She's a doctor.

21 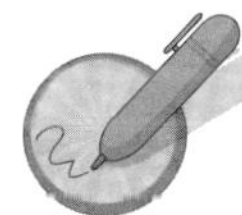 Write.

This is my sister.

 Are you ready for Unit 4?

4 My body

1 Write. Then number.

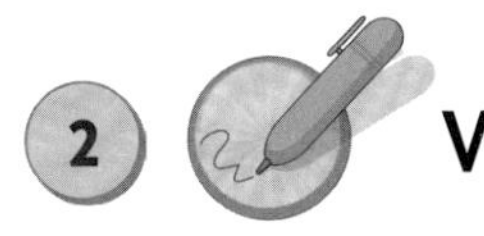

2 Write. Then circle.

1  feet

a  b  c 

2 wings

a  b  c 

3 tail

a  b  c 

4 arms

a 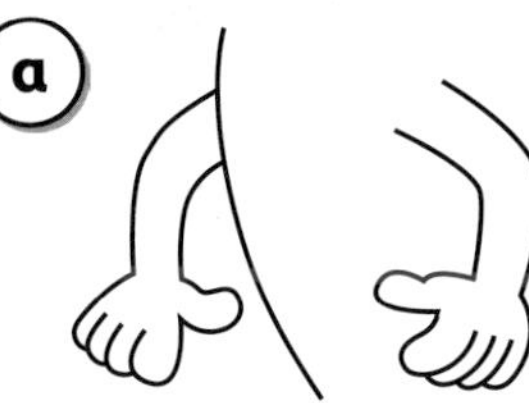 b 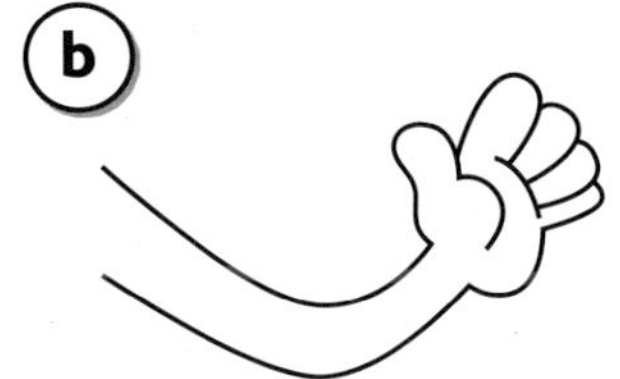 c 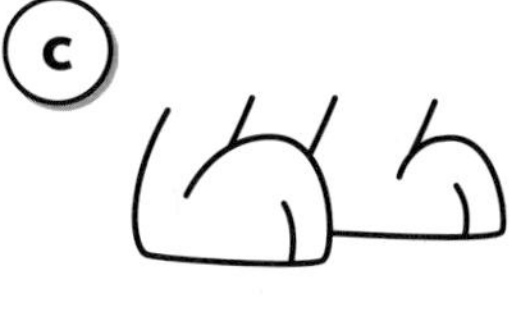

3 Listen and circle. Then color.

1 I have a (pink / purple) body.

2 I have (brown / orange) hands.

3 I have (yellow / blue) feet.

 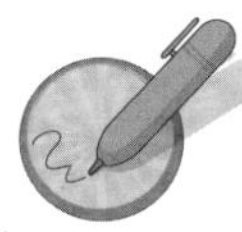

4 Count and write.

I have three legs.

1 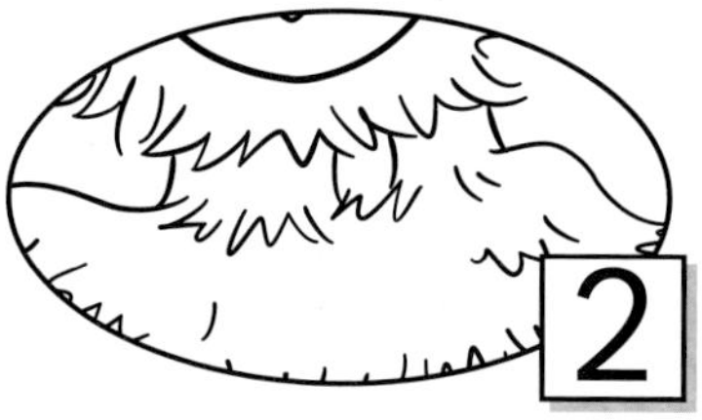 2 necks

2  shoulders

3  elbows

4  fingers

5 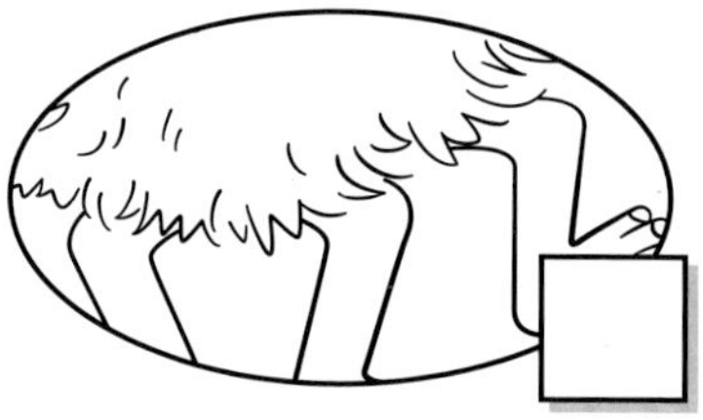 knees

6  toes

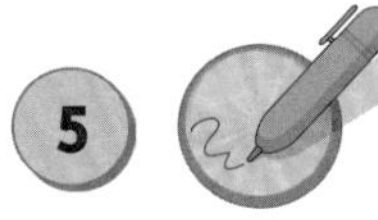

5 Look at Activity 4. Read and ✓ or ✗.

1 I have three knees. 

2 I have eight toes. 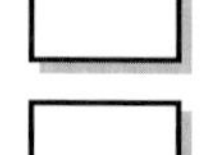

3 I have two heads. 

4 I have four arms. 

Lesson 3 37 Sing. (See Student Book page 46.)

 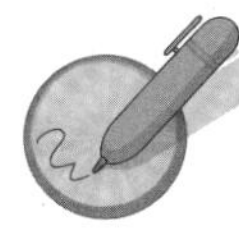

Read and circle. Then color.

1 I have a (foot / feet).

(It's / They're) green.

2 I have three (finger / fingers).

(It's / They're) pink.

3 I have five (leg / legs).

(It's / They're) brown.

4 I have a (body / head).

(It's / They're) orange.

 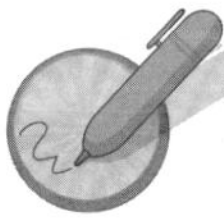

Write. Then color.

I have one head. It's red.

I have six arms. They're black.

I have four feet. They're blue.

I have eight toes. They're yellow.

 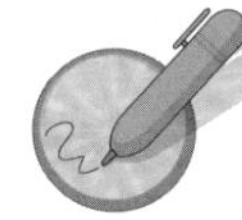 **Draw and write.**

1 I have ☐ heads.

2 I have ☐ arms.

3 I have ☐ legs.

9 Listen and draw.

 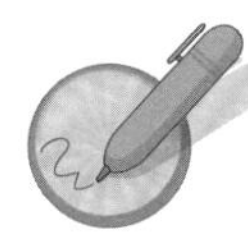 **Look and ✓ = clean or ✗ = not clean.**

1

2

  **Draw and write.**

MY BODY is not clean.

MY BODY is clean.

 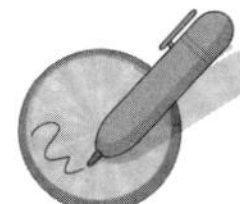 **Look and circle.**

1. I have (dirty / clean) hands.
2. I have dirty (feet / hands).
3. Wash your (hands / feet).
4. Wash your (hands / feet).
5. I have (dirty / clean) hands.
6. I have clean (hands / feet).

 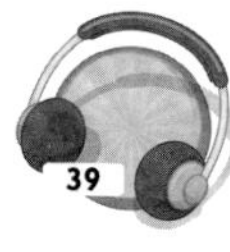

Listen and check your answers.

 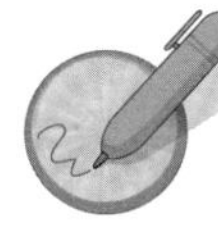 **Read the words. Circle the pictures.**

kick kid neck sock

15 Listen to the sounds and circle the letters.

1 k e i a

2 d t k e

3 a e k o

4 a i ck g

16  Listen and write the letters.

1 ______ 2 ______ 3 ______

17  Listen and write the words.

1 _ i t 2 p _ n 3 p _ t 4 t _ n

 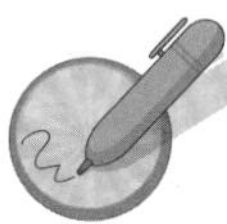 Draw. Then count and write.

I have two heads.

1 ☐ necks
2 ☐ arms
3 ☐ hands
4 ☐ fingers
5 ☐ legs
6 ☐ feet
7 ☐ toes

19 Look and find. Then color the picture in Activity 18.

1 heads 2 body 3 arms 4 legs 5 toes

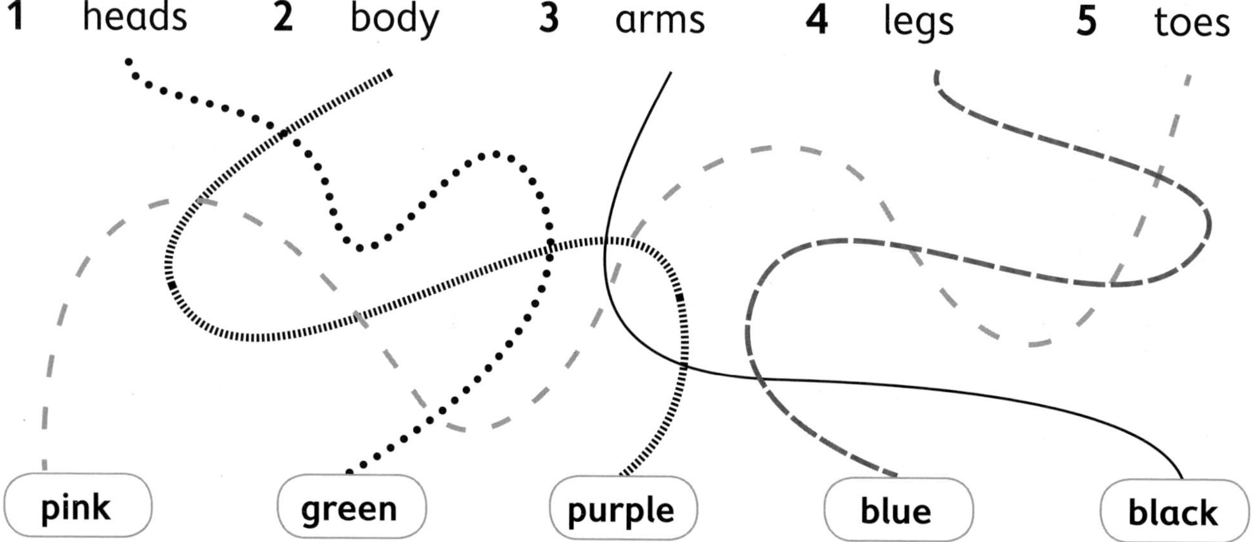

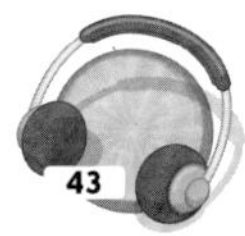

20 Listen and color.

1
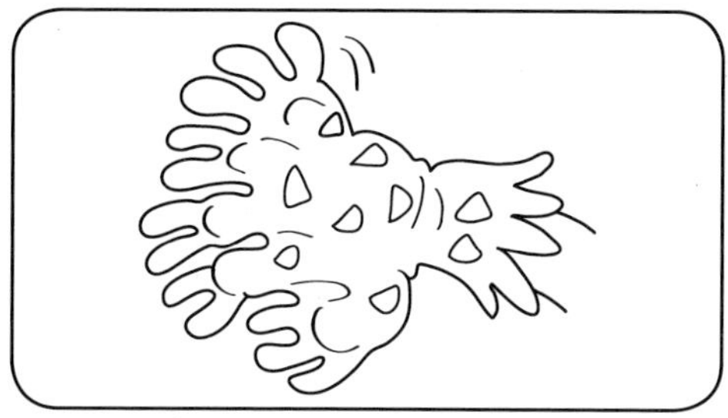

2
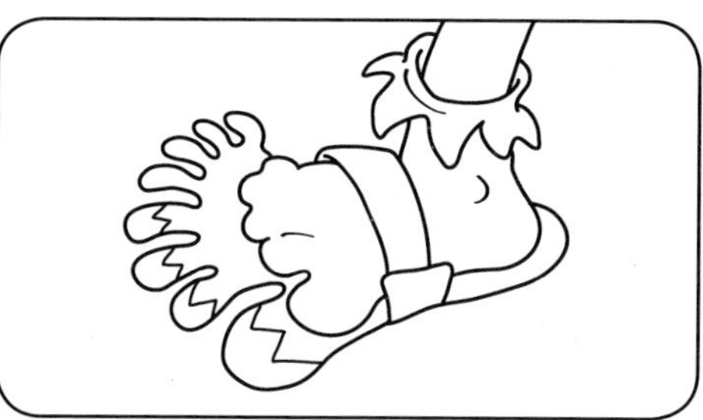

3

4

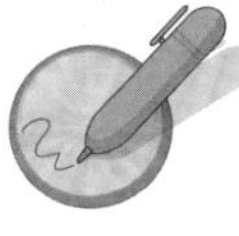

21 Find and circle.

body
elbow
fingers
foot
hand
knee
shoulders
toes

G	Q	B	E	I	T	X	H	B	P
I	J	E	F	I	N	G	E	R	S
R	N	L	J	H	K	L	M	R	E
K	E	F	I	E	G	N	E	F	L
F	U	D	O	F	K	D	H	I	B
W	V	W	L	O	L	A	T	S	O
B	O	D	Y	U	T	O	E	Z	W
L	V	V	O	D	O	O	T	E	S
H	T	H	L	E	T	H	A	N	D
V	S	I	O	P	Z	J	S	U	A

Are you ready for Unit 5?

5 Pets

  Look and write.

cat dog frog hamster mouse parrot rabbit snake turtle

1 

____

2 

____

3 

____

4 

____

5 

____

6 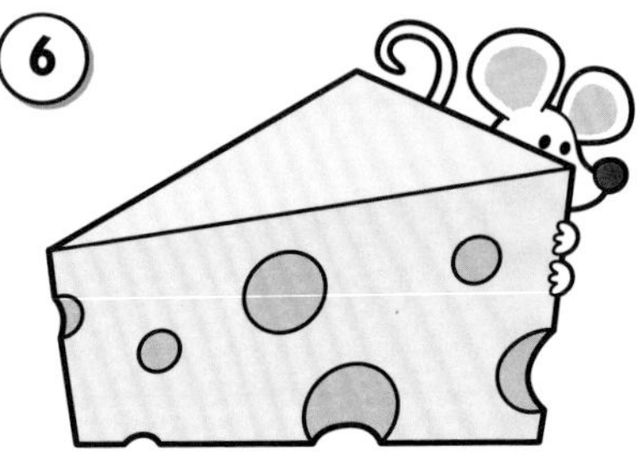

____

7 

____

8 

____

9 

____

2  Listen and circle.

3 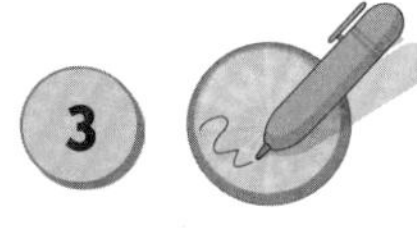 Circle and write.

cat hamster parrot

1 I (have / has) a ________________.

2 She (have / has) a ________________.

3 He (have / has) a ________________.

 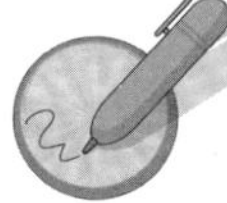

Look and write.

big old short small tall young

1

small

2

3

4

5

6

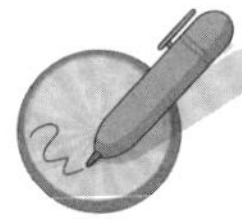

5 Number. Then circle.

1 (He / She) has a rabbit.
2 (He / She) has a frog.
3 (He / She) has a dog.
4 (He / She) has a cat.

 46 Sing. (See Student Book page 58.)

6 47 **Listen, look, and check (✓).**

1 Yes, he does. ☐
No, he doesn't. ☐

2 Yes, she does. ☐
No, she doesn't. ☐

3 Yes, he does. ☐
No, he doesn't. ☐

4 Yes, she does. ☐
No, she doesn't. ☐

5 Yes, he does. ☐
No, he doesn't. ☐

6 Yes, she does. ☐
No, she doesn't. ☐

7 48 **Listen and number.**

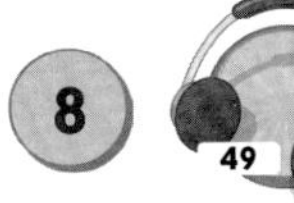

8 Listen and number.

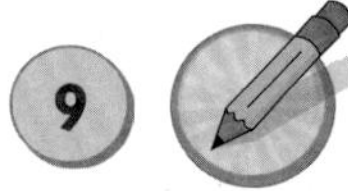

9 Draw and check (✓).

1 He has a dog. ☐

He has a mouse. ☐

2 He has a cat. ☐

He has a rabbit. ☐

 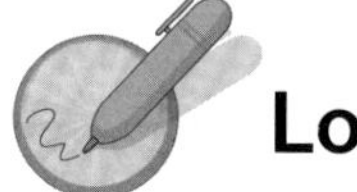

10 Look and match.

1 

2 

3 

a 

b 

c d 

e 

f 

4 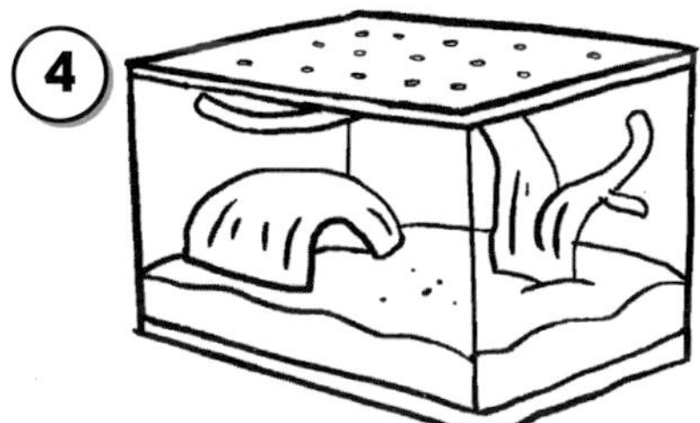

5 

6 

11 Draw a pet you take care of.

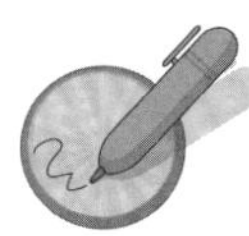

Write. Then match.

chick kitten puppy

1 

2 

3 

______ ______ ______

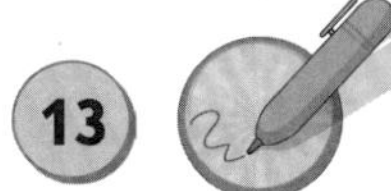

Connect the dots. Then circle.

1 

It's a (kitten / puppy / chick).

2 

It's a (kitten / puppy / chick).

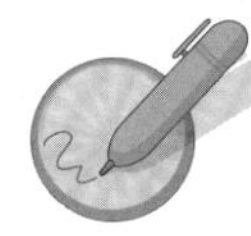

Read the words. Circle the pictures.

PHONICS

b h r u

bag cup hat rat

15 Listen to the sounds and circle the letters.

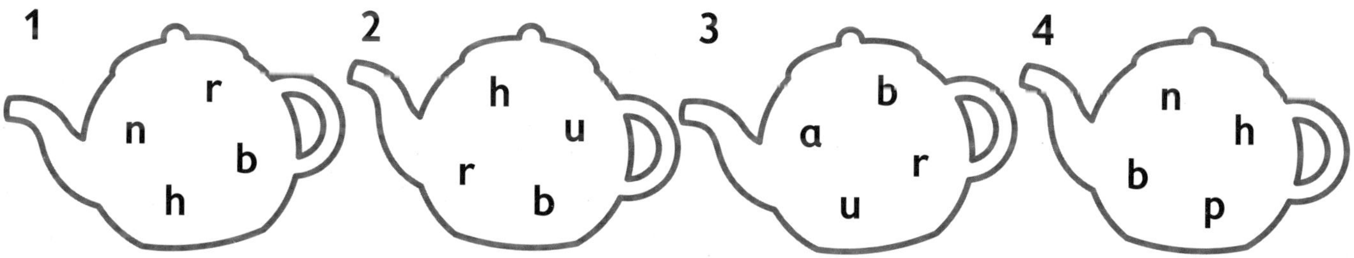

16 Listen and write the letters.

1 ______ 2 ______ 3 ______ 4 ______

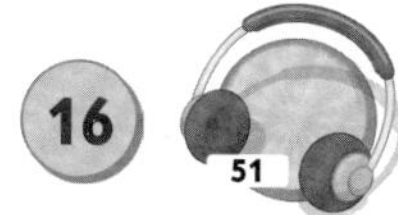

17 Listen and write the words.

1 __ p 2 __ __ d 3 __ o __ 4 t __ __

 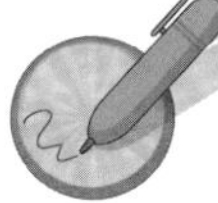 **Look and circle.**

1

I have a(n) (young / old) dog.

2

I have a (tall / short) dog.

3

I have a (short / long) snake.

4

I have a (big / small) turtle.

19 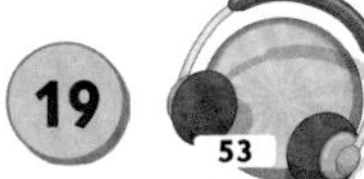

Listen and check (✓).

1

2

3

4

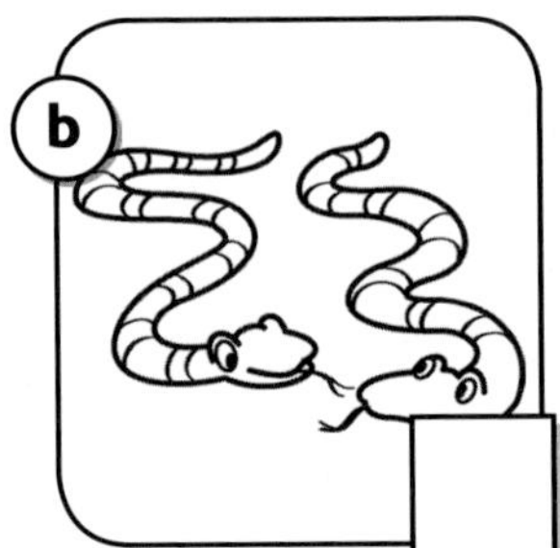

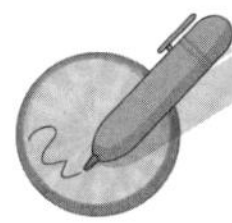

Look and write.

cat dog frog hamster mouse parrot rabbit turtle

He has a __________, a __________, a __________, and a __________.

She has a __________, a __________, a __________, and a __________.

Read and draw.

1

I have a cat.

2

Does she have a parrot?

Yes, she does.

3

Do you have a hamster?

No, I don't. I have a snake.

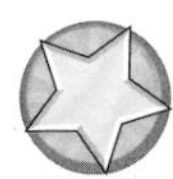

Are you ready for Unit 6?

6 My house

1 Draw. Then write.

bathroom bedroom dining room
door kitchen living room window

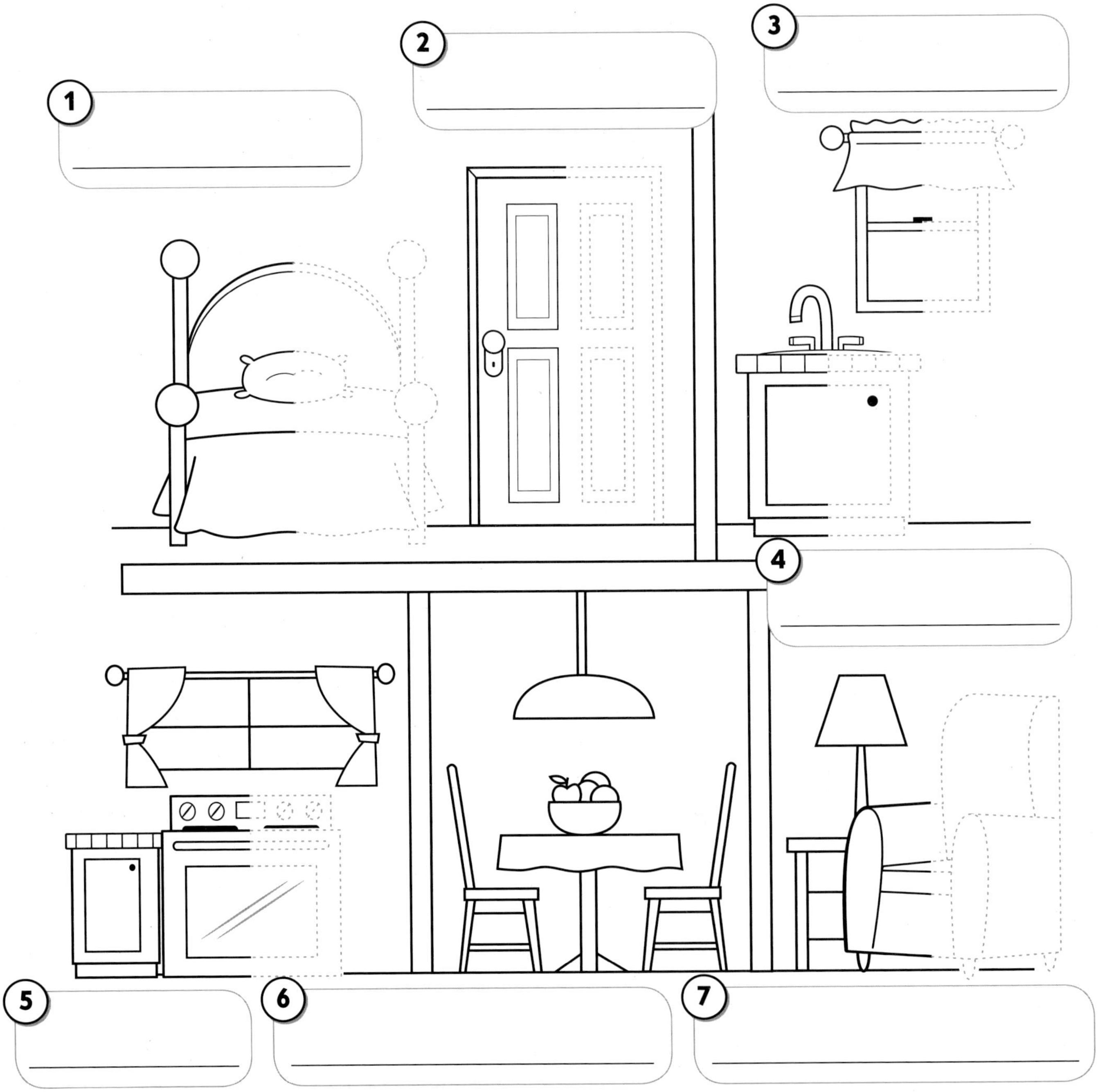

1 ______

2 ______

3 ______

4 ______

5 ______

6 ______

7 ______

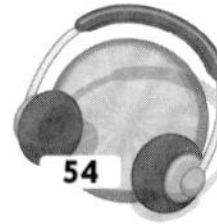

Listen and number. Then match.

She's in the bathroom.
He's in the dining room.
They're in the kitchen.
They're in the living room.

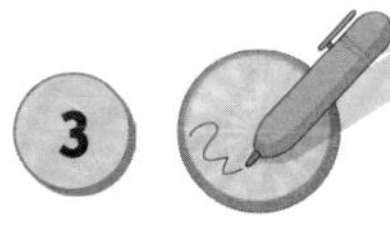

3 Connect the dots. Then read and circle.

1 (Where's / Where are) Waldo?

2 He's in the (dining room / living room).

4 

Listen and number.

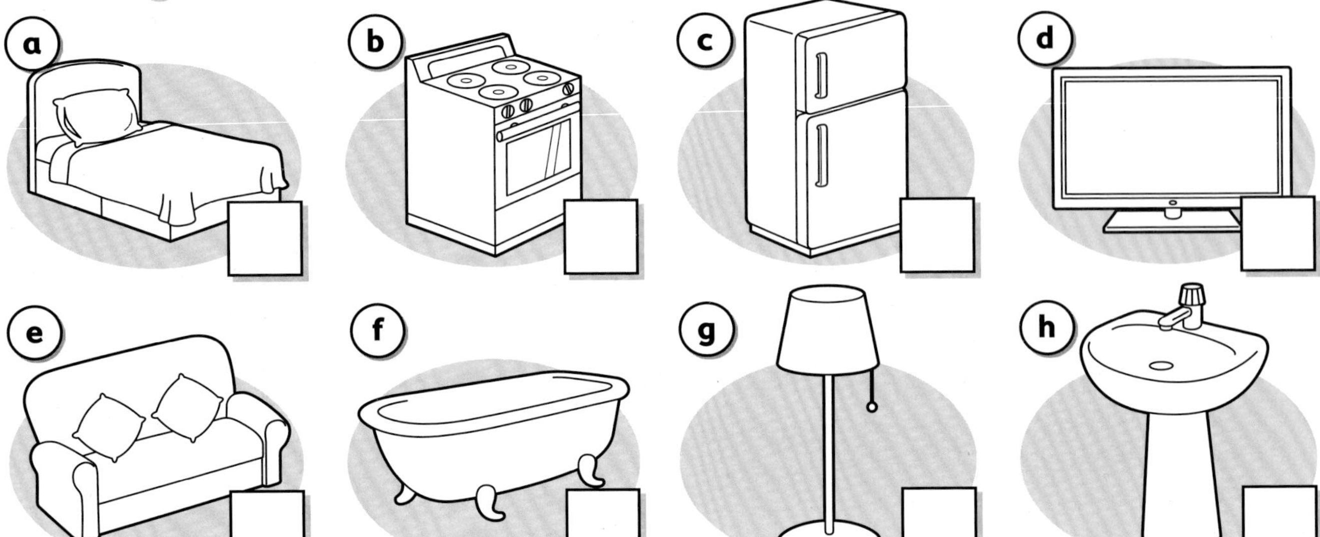

5 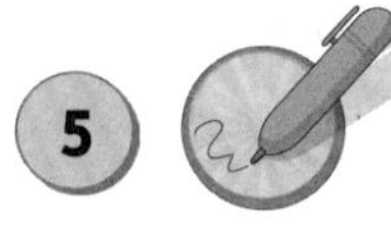
Look, read, and circle.

1 They're in the (bathroom / bedroom).

2 They're in the (living room / bathroom).

3 They're in the (yard / kitchen).

Lesson 3 57 **Sing.** (See Student Book page 68.)

Read and find. Then circle and write.

bed bedroom ~~dining room~~
refrigerator sofa table tub

1 (There's / There are) a bird in the dining room.

2 (There's / There are) two rabbits in the ______.

3 (There's / There are) a teddy bear in the ______.

4 (There's / There are) two dogs under the ______.

5 (There's / There are) books on the ______.

6 (There's / There are) a boy on the ______.

7 (There's / There are) a cat in the ______.

Listen and ✓ or ✗.

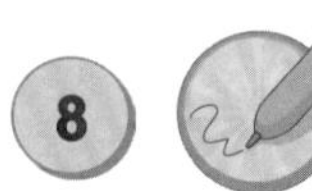

Read and circle.

He's in the (kitchen / living room).

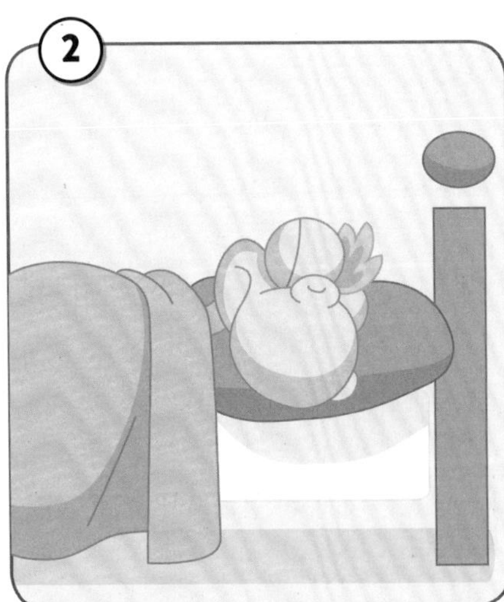

He's in the (bedroom / dining room).

He's in the (kitchen / bathroom).

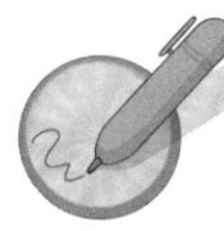

Look and match.

VALUES

Be neat.

10 Draw.

My house

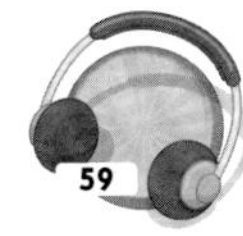

Write. Then listen and follow the path.

house	library	playground	store	zoo

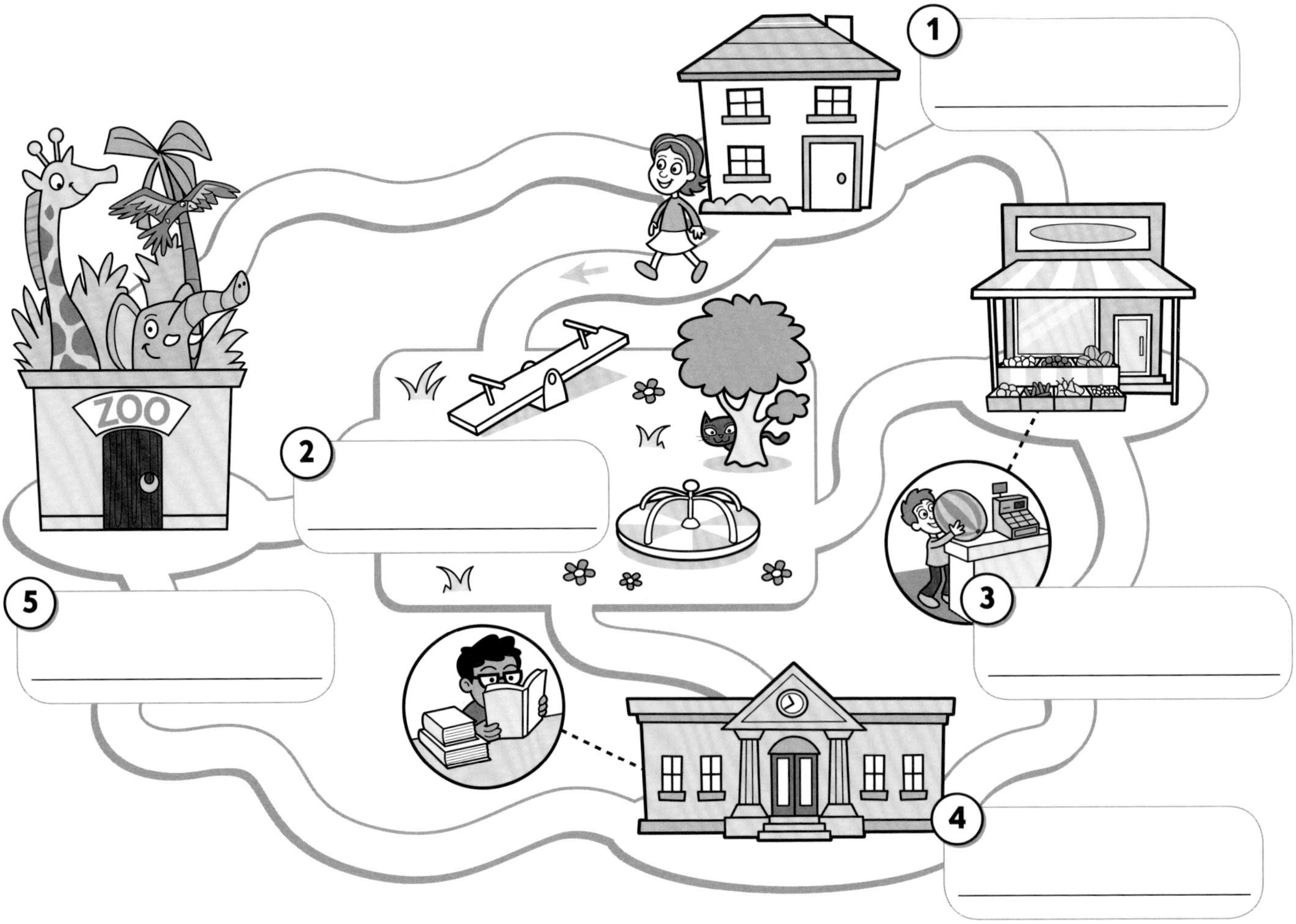

1 ______

2 ______

3 ______

4 ______

5 ______

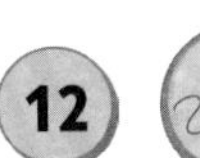
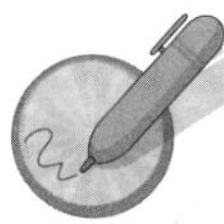

Circle.

1 She's at the (zoo / playground).

2 It's in the (store / yard).

3 He's in the (library / house).

PHONICS

13 Read the words. Circle the pictures.

bell doll fan leg

14 Listen to the sounds and circle the letters.

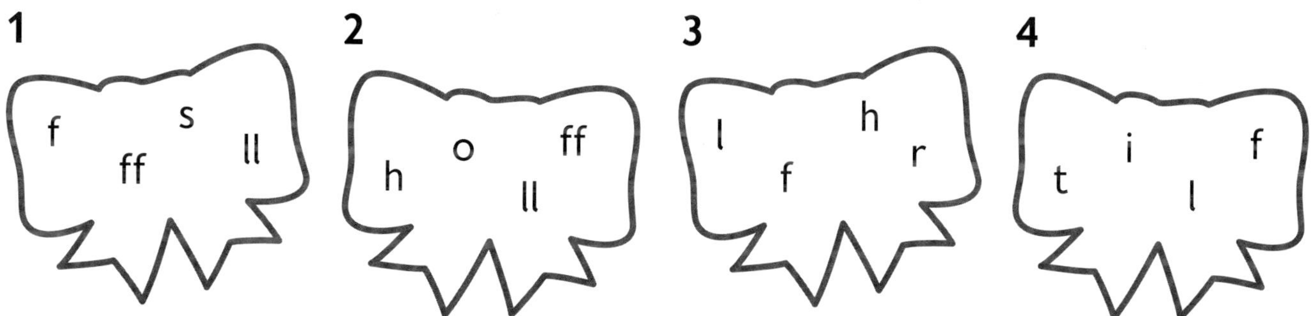

15 Listen and write the letters.

1 ____ 2 ____ 3 ____ 4 ____

16 Listen and write the words.

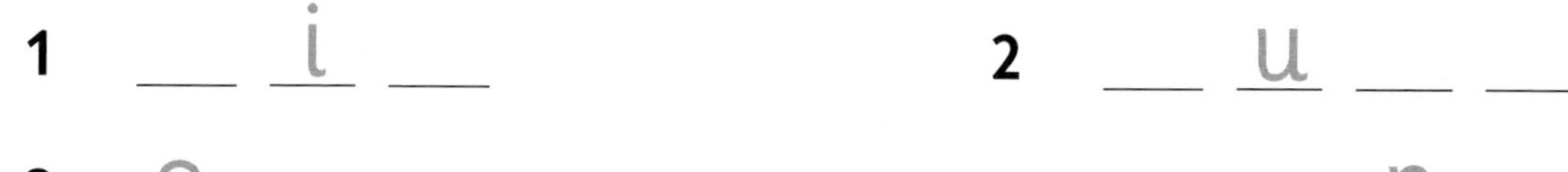

1 ___ i ___

2 ___ u ___ ___

3 o ___ ___

4 ___ ___ p

 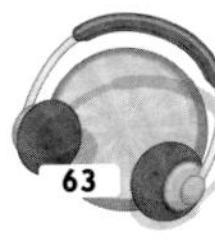 Listen and draw.

1
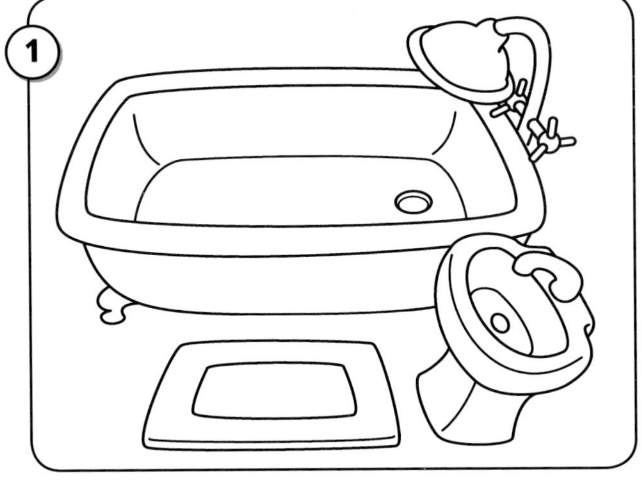

2

3

4

18 Look at Activity 17. Write.

1 There's a [u t b] ________________ in the bathroom.

2 There's a [f a s o] ________________ in the living room.

3 There's a [i w n d w o] ________________ in the dining room.

4 There's a [e b d] ________________ in the bedroom.

5 There's a [k i n s] ________________ in the bathroom.

6 There's a [v t] ________________ in the living room.

 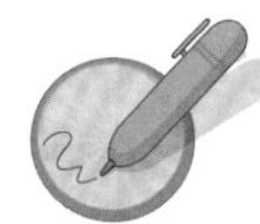

Read and write.

bathroom bedroom dining room
kitchen living room yard

1 He's in the ________________.

2 He's in the ________________.

3 She's in the ________________.

4 They're in the ________________.

5 She's in the ________________.

6 They're in the ________________.

 **Are you ready for Unit 7?**

7 Food

 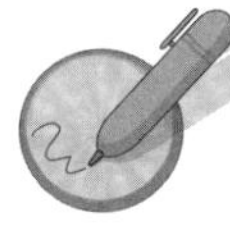 **Draw. Then write.**

bread	cake	cheese	fish	fruit	milk	salad	yogurt

1 

____

2 

____

3 

____

4 

____

5 

____

6 

____

7 

____

8 

____

  What does Cody like? Find, color, and check (✓).

salad	☐
fish	☐
yogurt	☐
fruit	☐
bread	☐
milk	☐
cheese	☐
cake	☐

  Read and draw.

 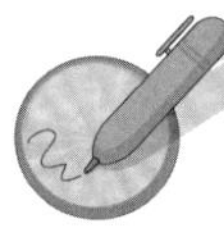 **Look and number.**

honey	☐	cake	☐	jello	☐	bread	☐
ice cream	☐	meat	☐	chocolate	☐	juice	☐

5 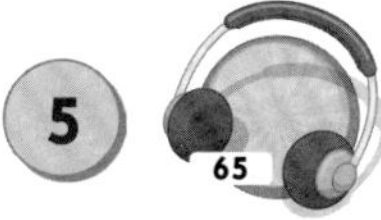 **Listen and number. Then circle and write.**

1 I (like / don't like) ____________.

2 I (like / don't like) ____________.

3 I (like / don't like) ____________.

4 I (like / don't like) ____________.

cheese
honey
jello
meat

 66 **Sing.** (See Student Book page 80.)

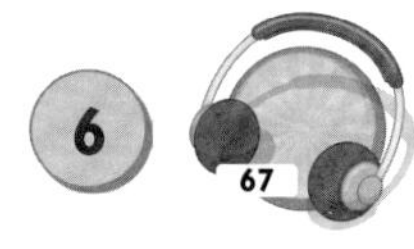

6 Listen and number.

a

b

c

d

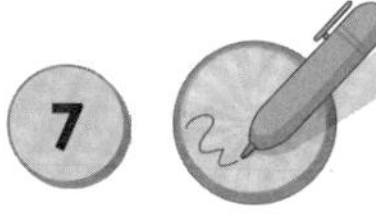

7 Look and write.

1

Do you like jello?

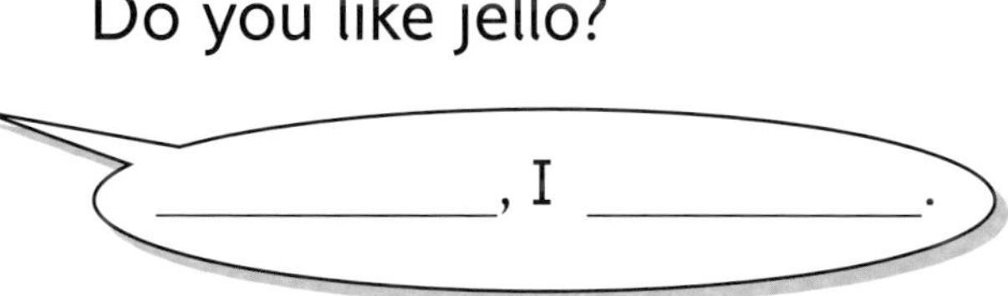

2

Do you like honey?

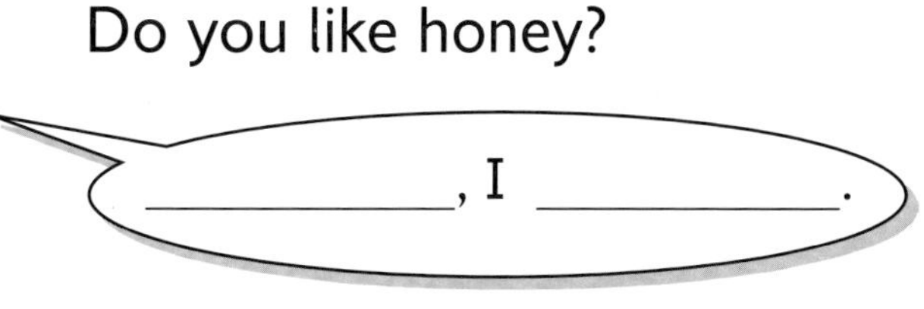

 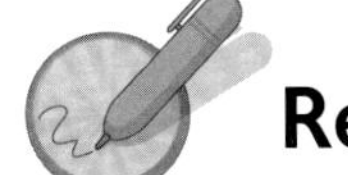

8 Read and match.

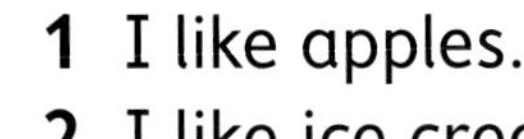

a 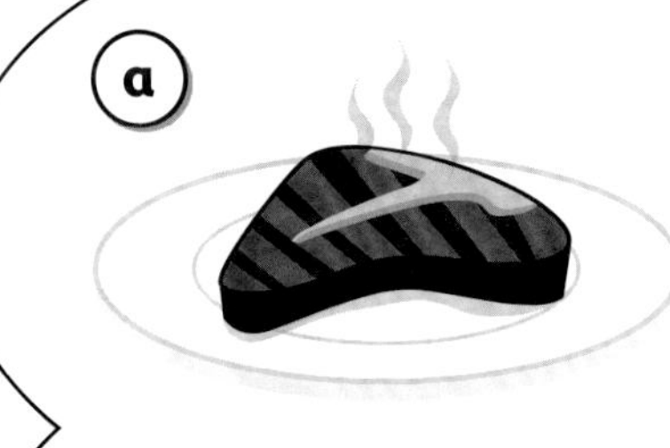

b 

c 

d 

9 Look and draw.

 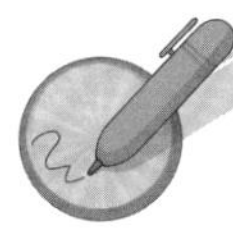 Look and write.

Goodbye! Happy birthday!
Hello! I'm sorry. Thank you.

1

2

3

4

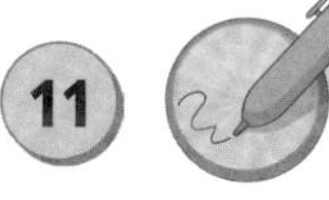 Draw and write.

 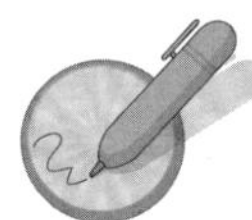 **Find and write.**

cake chocolate salad

13 **Check (✓). Then draw.**

It's healthy!

- fruit ☐
- salad ☐
- cake ☐
- bread ☐
- yogurt ☐
- milk ☐
- juice ☐
- chocolate ☐

PHONICS

j ss v w

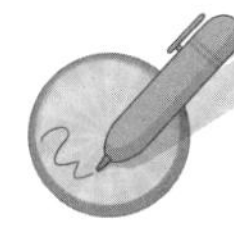

Read the words. Circle the pictures.

jet kiss van wig

15 Listen to the sounds and circle the letters.

68

1 v ss c f

2
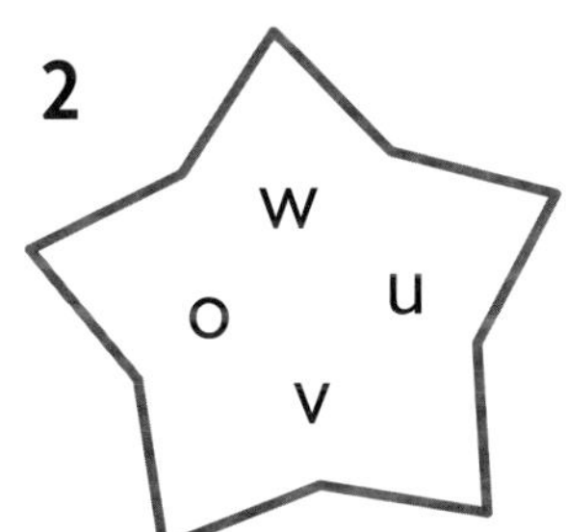

3
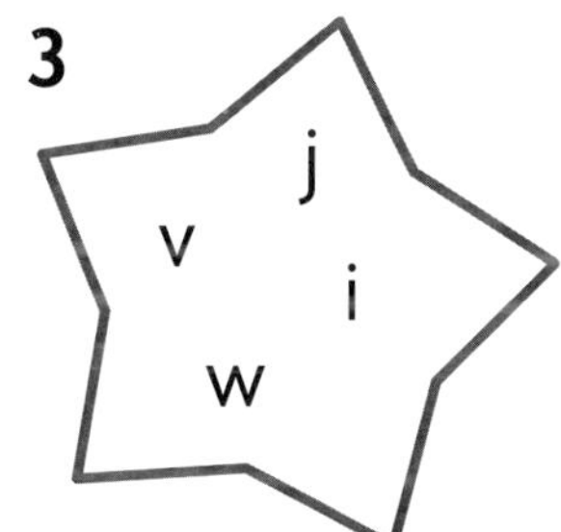

4
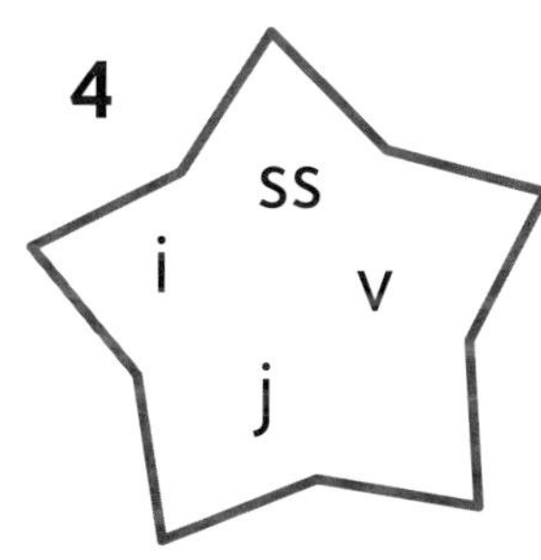

16 Listen and write the letters.

69

1 ____ 2 ____ 3 ____ 4 ____

17 Listen and write the words.

70

1 m ___ ___ ___

2 ___ ___ t

3 ___ ___ m

4 ___ e ___

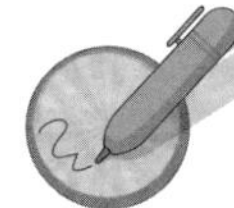

18 Look and write.

bread honey jello juice
meat milk yogurt

1

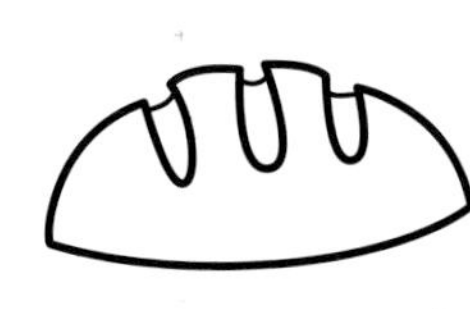

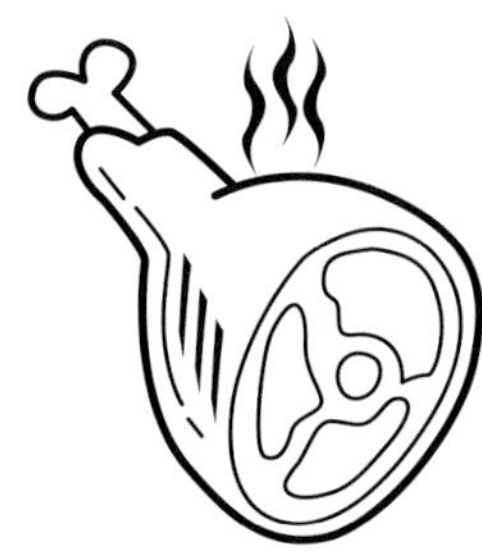
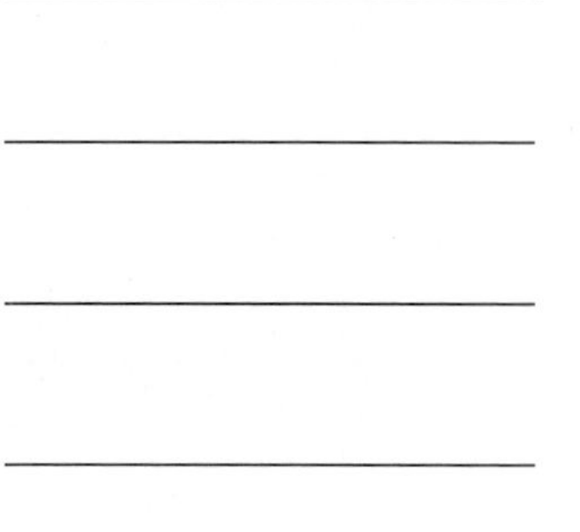

I like...

bread

______

______

______

2

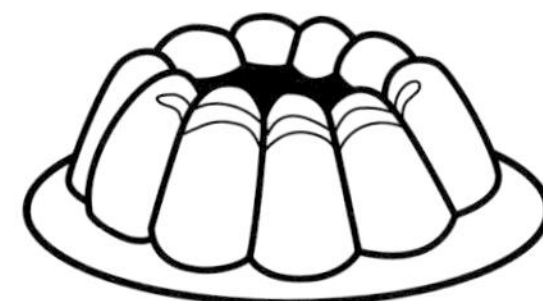

I don't like...

______

______

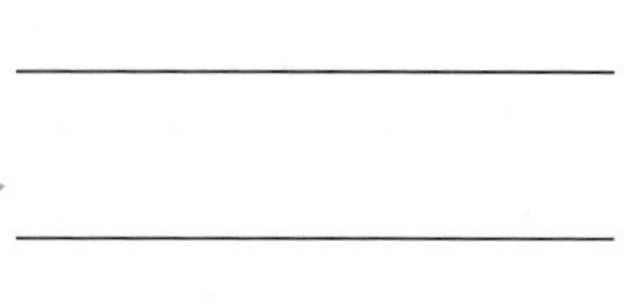

______

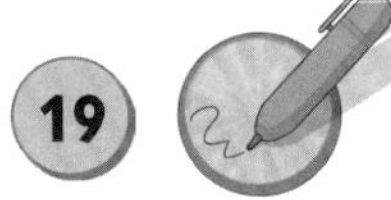

19 Look and write.

I like ______.

Listen and ✓ = likes or ✗ = dislikes.

1  ☐

2  ☐

3  ☐

4 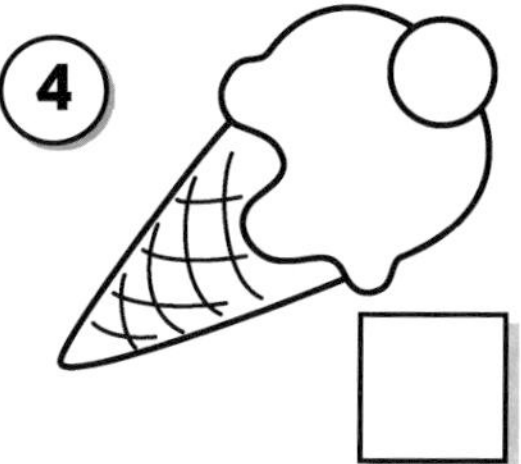 ☐

5  ☐

6  ☐

7 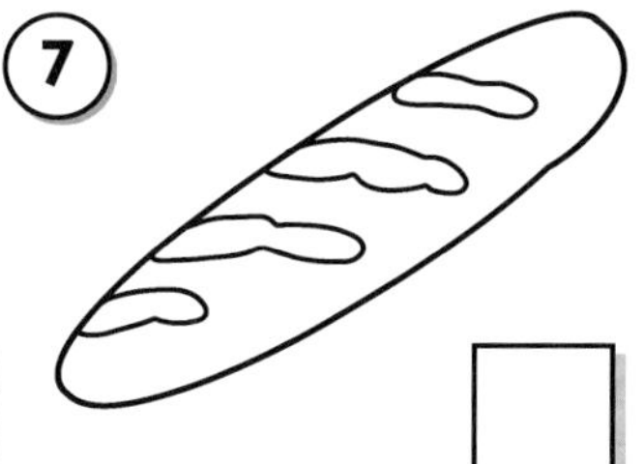 ☐

8  ☐

Listen, draw, and match.

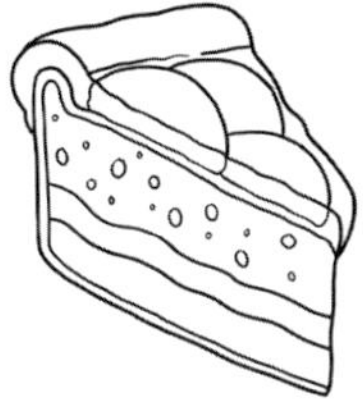

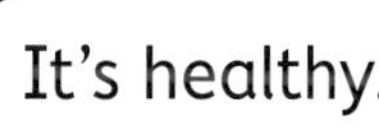

4

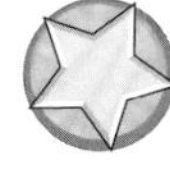

Are you ready for Unit 8?

8 I'm happy!

1 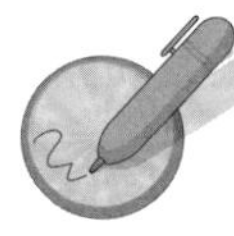 Look and write.

happy hungry scared thirsty tired

I'm ______________.

I'm ______________.

I'm ______________.

I'm ______________.

I'm ______________.

2 Listen and ✓ or ✗.

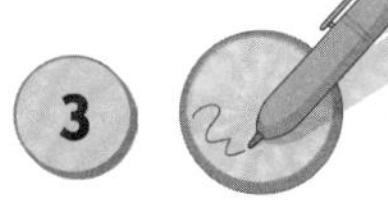

3 Find and circle.

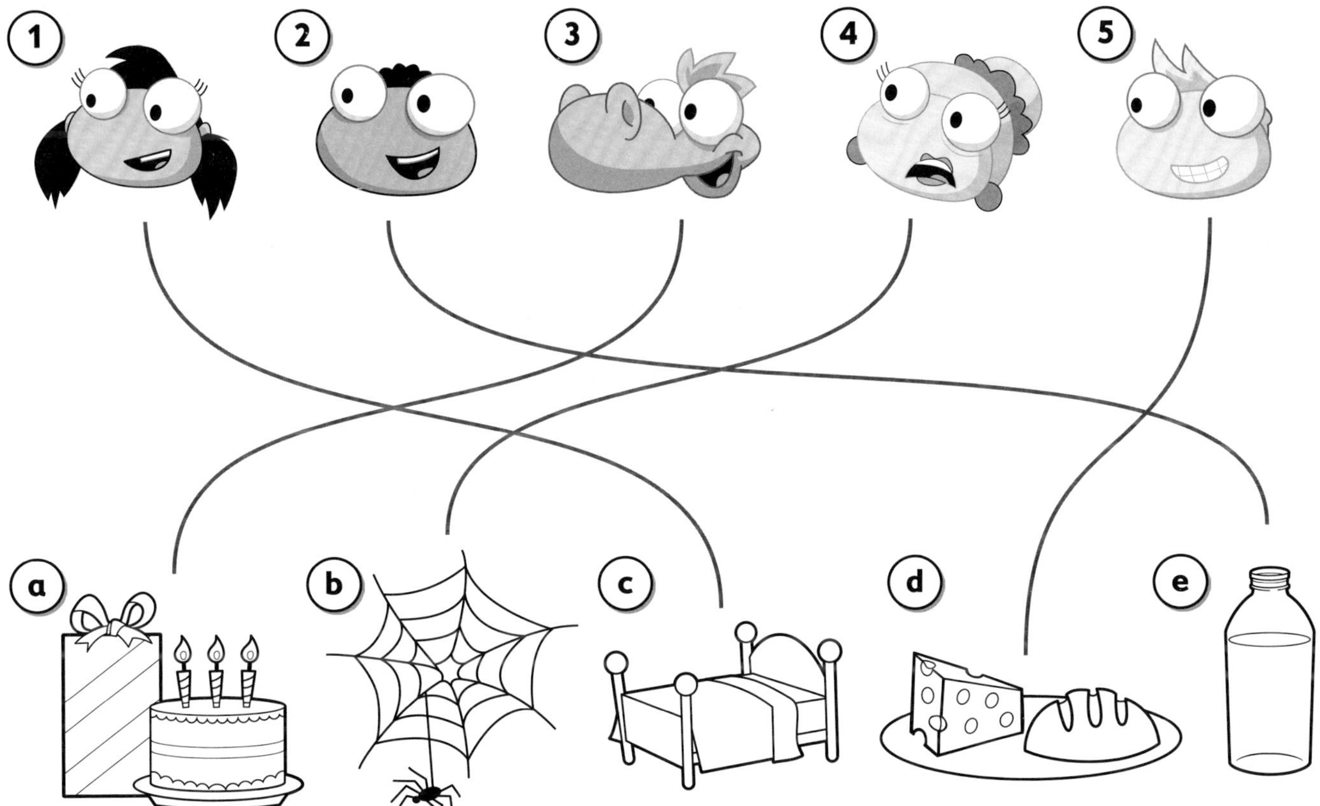

1 She's (happy / tired).

2 He's (thirsty / tired).

3 He's (happy / thirsty).

4 She's (scared / hungry).

5 He's (happy / hungry).

 74 Chant. (See Student Book page 89.)

 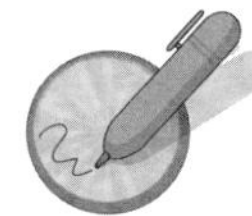

Look and write.

angry bored cold hot hurt sad sick

He's ________.

He's ________.

She's ________.

She's ________.

He's ________.

She's ________.

He's ________.

5 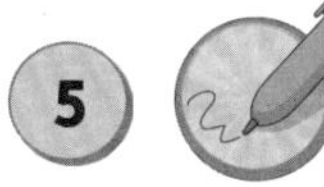

Match.

a stamp

b snap

c clap

d turn around

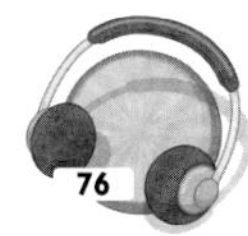

6 Listen and number.

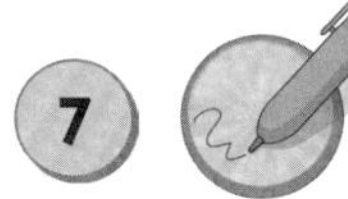

7 Look and write.

Yes, he is. Yes, I am. No, I'm not. No, she isn't.

1

Are you sad?

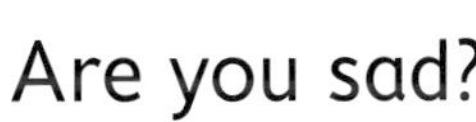

____

2

Are you cold?

____

I'm hot.

3

Is she angry?

____

She's bored.

4

Is he hurt?

____

Listen and number.

a

b

c

d

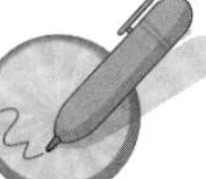

Draw and write.

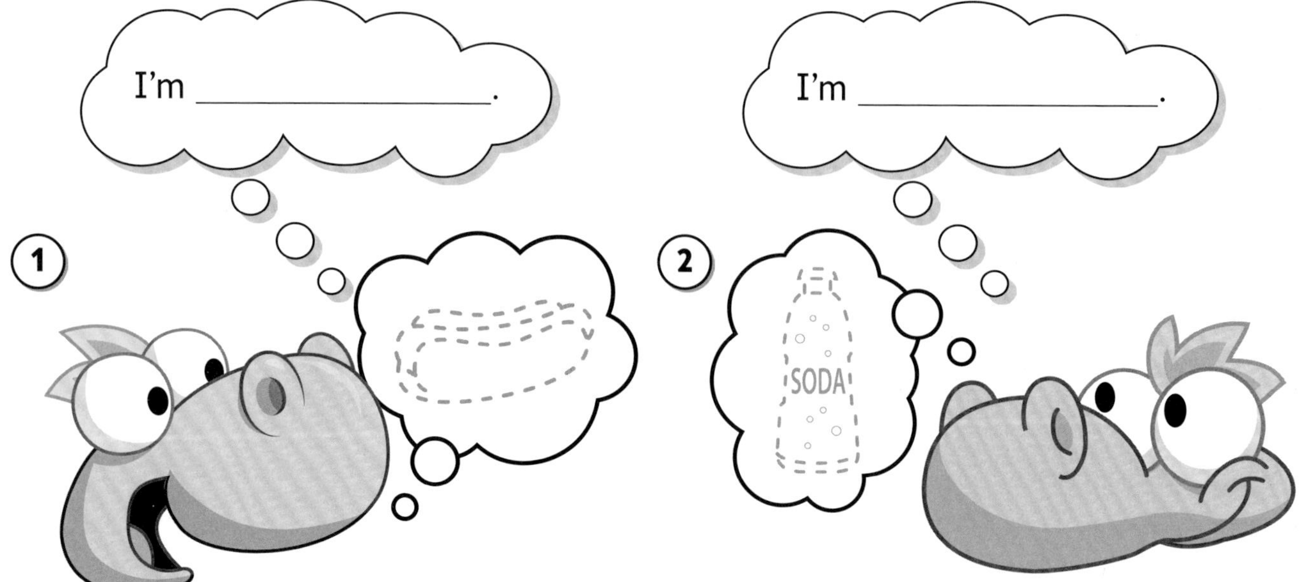

Listen and number.

Draw and write.

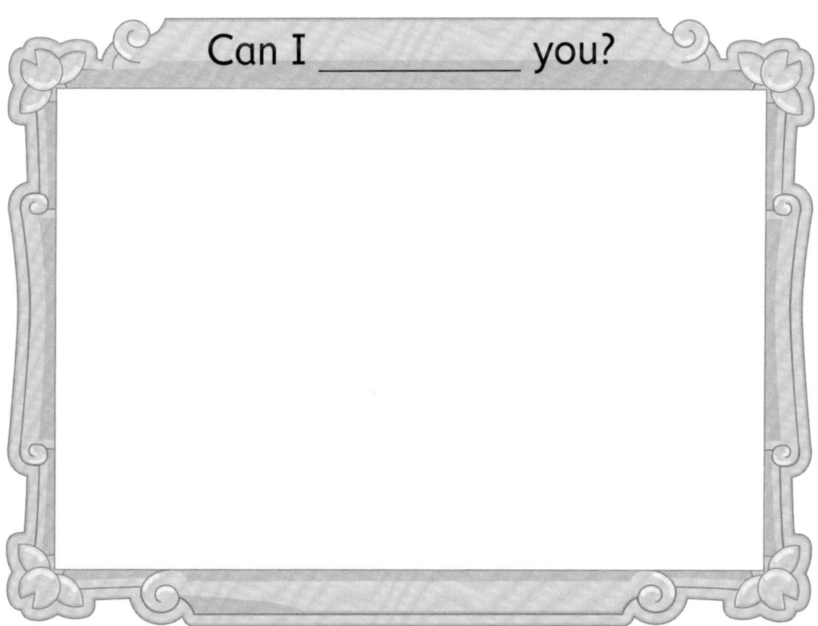

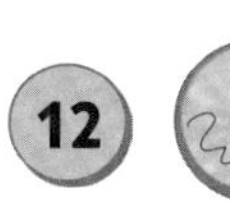 

12 Look and match.

1

2

It's hot.

It's cold.

3

4

13 Look and circle.

1

2

It's a (polar bear / penguin).

It's (hot / cold).

It's a (turtle / snake).

It's (hot / cold).

 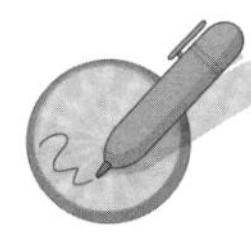 **Read the words. Circle the pictures.**

PHONICS

qu x y

z zz

box buzz taxi yes

  **Listen to the sounds and circle the letters.**

1

y z j x

2

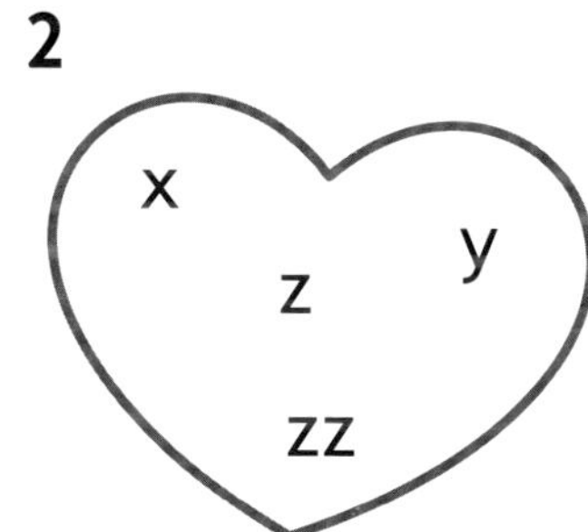

3

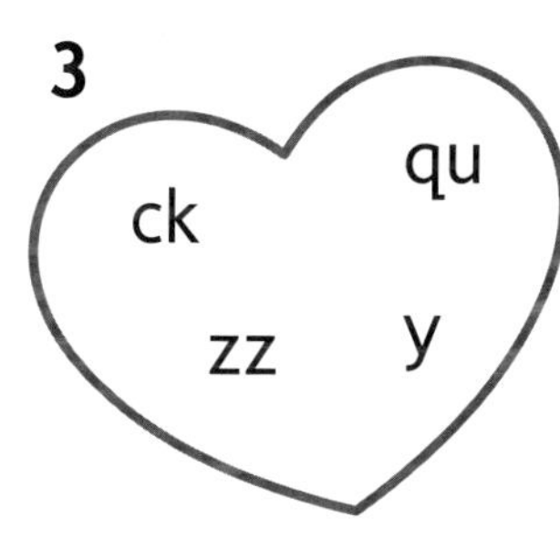

4

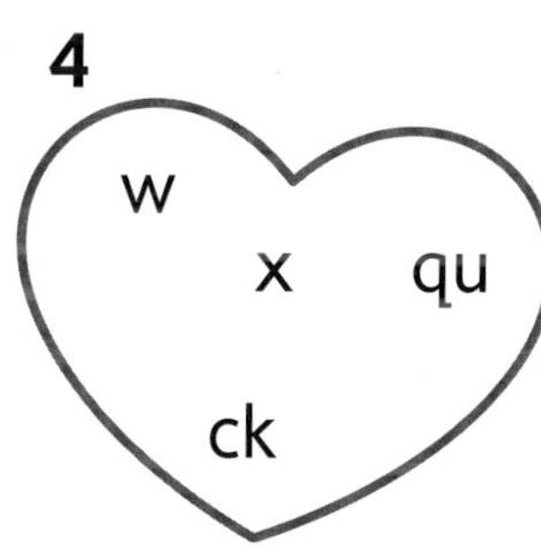

16 **Listen and write the letters.**

1 ____ 2 ____ 3 ____ 4 ____ 5 ____

17  **Listen and write the words.**

1 __ __ i __ 2 __ __ z __

3 __ __ p 4 __ __ l __

  Write.

angry bored cold hot hungry hurt sick thirsty

He's ______________.

He's ______________.

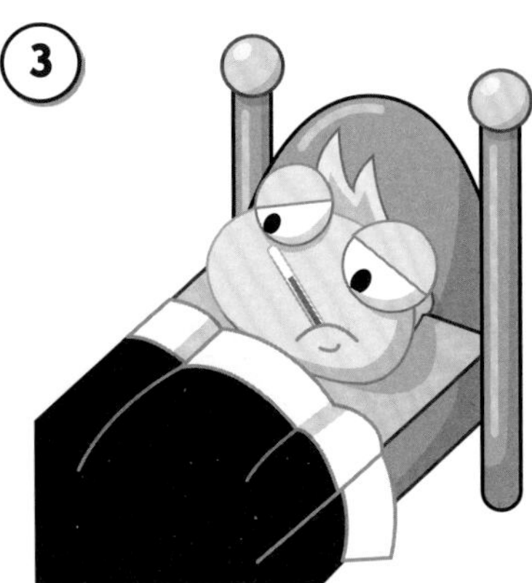

He's ______________.

She's ______________.

He's ______________.

She's ______________.

She's ______________.

He's ______________.

Listen and draw. Then circle.

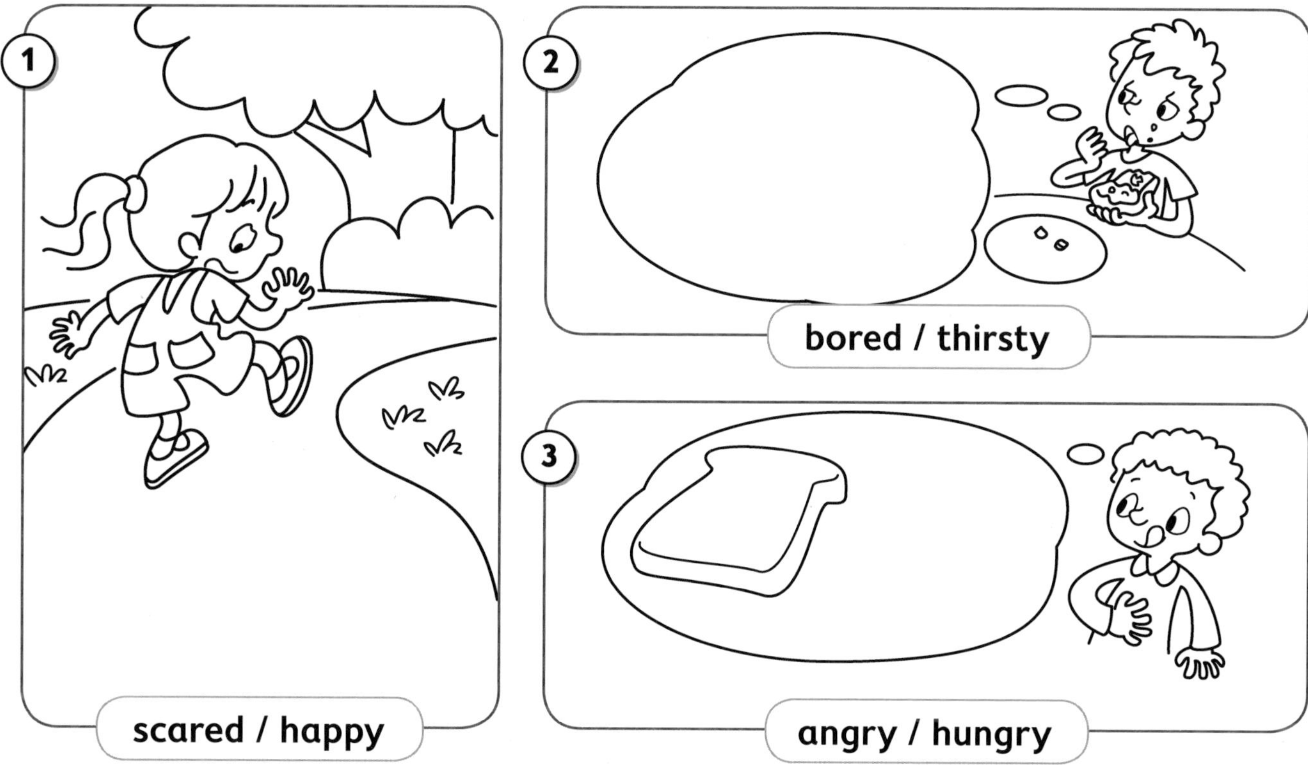

1 scared / happy

2 bored / thirsty

3 angry / hungry

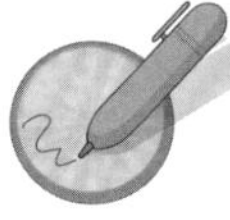

Find and circle.

angry
bored
cold
happy
hot
hungry
sad
sick
thirsty
tired

W	R	H	V	G	D	S	S	T	H
Q	U	S	U	L	K	S	Y	H	A
B	C	A	O	N	I	B	K	I	P
T	O	C	A	D	G	F	M	R	P
O	U	R	E	N	W	R	B	S	Y
R	T	R	E	W	G	D	Y	T	S
Q	I	A	S	D	A	R	I	Y	I
T	E	M	T	A	U	P	Y	J	C
A	U	M	U	G	D	U	F	W	K
T	L	P	K	Q	S	T	H	O	T

1  **Look and write.**

apple balloon bird cake door
hat photo tablet teddy bear

1 

____

2 

____

3 

____

4 

____

5 

____

6 

____

7 

____

8 

____

9 

____

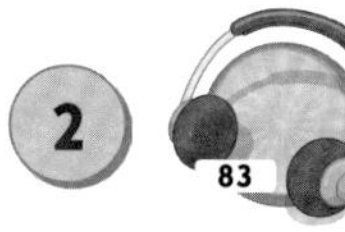

2 Listen and number.

a

b

c

d

e

f

g

h

i

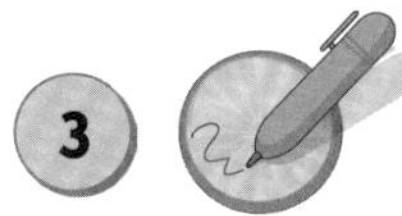

3 Look and write.

1

We like ________________.

2

I have two ________________.

3

This is my pet.
It's a ________________.

4

Do you like
________________?

Yes, I do.

4 Look, circle, and write.

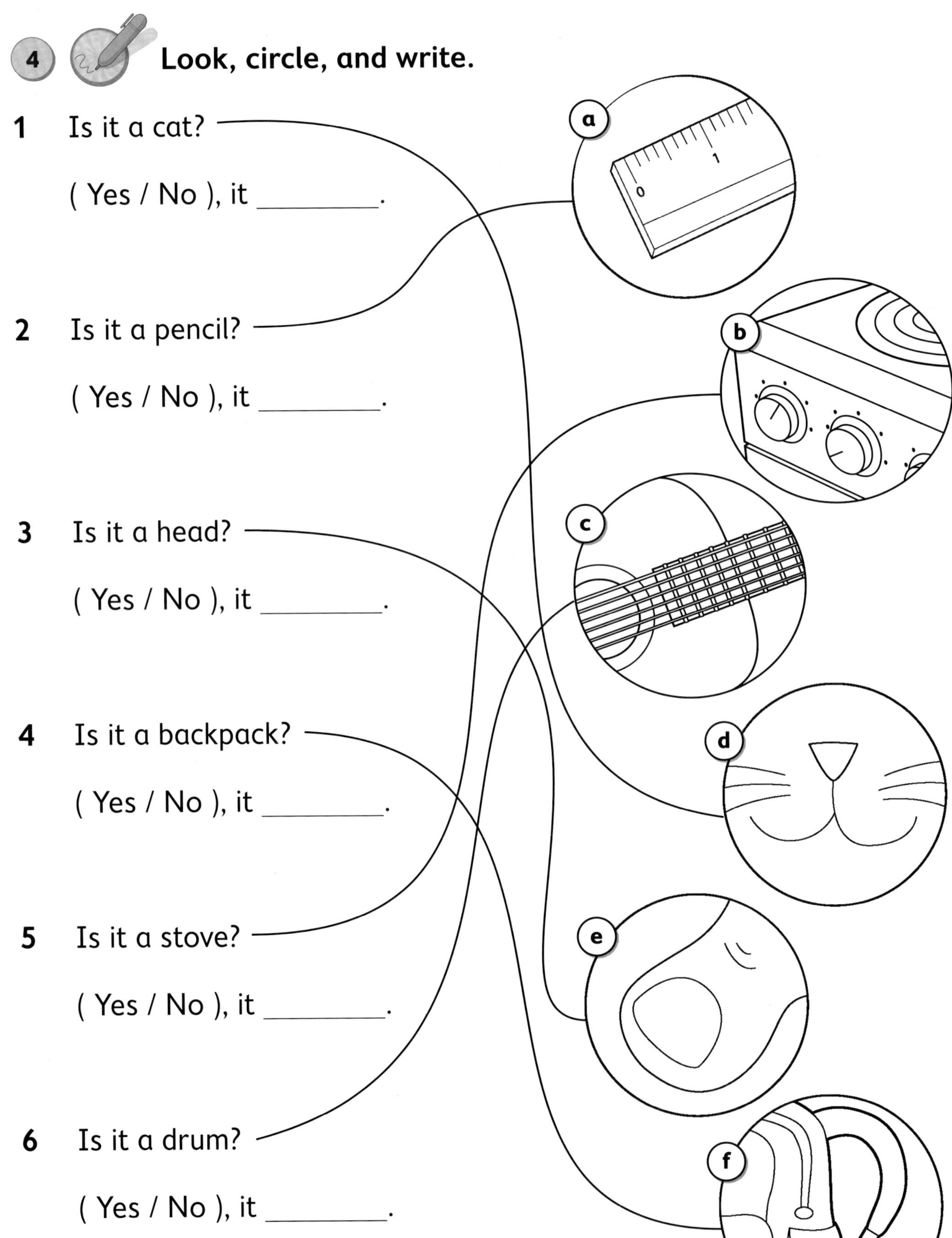

1 Is it a cat?

(Yes / No), it ________.

2 Is it a pencil?

(Yes / No), it ________.

3 Is it a head?

(Yes / No), it ________.

4 Is it a backpack?

(Yes / No), it ________.

5 Is it a stove?

(Yes / No), it ________.

6 Is it a drum?

(Yes / No), it ________.

5 Find and circle the one that doesn't belong. Then write.

1 cheese ruler meat salad ______

2 pencil book cat eraser ______

3 mom dad dancer sister ______

4 dog bed rabbit mouse ______

5 living room kitchen store bedroom ______

6 head sad happy angry ______

6 Read and answer.

1 How old are you? ______

2 What's your favorite food? ______

3 Do you have a pet? ______

4 What's your favorite color? ______

Welcome

Hello. I'm Mandy.	**Goodbye**.
I'm = I am	

Unit 1 My birthday

What's your name?	**My name's** Cody.
How old are you?	**I'm** seven.
What's = What is	

Is it purple?	Yes, **it is**. / No, **it isn't**.
What color is it?	**It's** pink.
isn't = is not	**It's = It is**

Unit 2 At school

What's this?	**It's** a book. **It's** red.
	It's a red book.

Are they blue?	Yes, **they are**.
	No, **they aren't**.
What color are they?	**They're** white.
aren't = are not	**They're = They are**

Unit 3 **My family**

This is my brother/sister.	
How old is he/she?	**He's/She's** nine.
He's = He is **She's = She is**	

Is he/she	a vet?	Yes, **he/she is**.
	an artist?	No, **he/she isn't**. **He's/She's** a cook.

Unit 4 **My body**

I **have**	a green tail.
	green arms.

I **have**	a head. It's yellow.
	three arms. They're red.

Unit 5 **Pets**

I have a dog.	**He/She has** a dog.

Do you	**have** a parrot?	Yes, I **do**.
		No, I **don't**.
Does he/she		Yes, he/she **does**.
		No, he/she **doesn't**. He/She **has** a big dog.
don't = do not **doesn't = does not**		

Unit 6 **My house**

Where's Aunt Fifi?	**She's** in the living room.
Where are Waldo and Beth?	**They're** in the bedroom.
Where's = Where is	

There's a lamp on the desk.
There are two kittens under the sofa.
There's = There is

Unit 7 **Food**

I like cake and milk.
I don't like salad and fish.

Do you like honey?	Yes, **I do**.
	No, **I don't**.

Unit 8 **I'm happy!**

I'm hungry.	**He's/She's** thirsty.

Are you happy?	Yes, **I am**.
	No, **I'm not**.
Is he/she happy?	Yes, **he/she is**.
	No, **he/she isn't**.